Girl in the
Tunnel

Maureen Sullivan grew up in Carlow town. When she was just twelve years old she was placed in the Magdalene Laundry at New Ross, County Wexford, where she was forced to work long hours scrubbing floors and washing clothes, and denied an education. After two years she was transferred to another laundry in Athy, County Kildare and then to a school for blind people in Dublin. After she left the school, she returned to Carlow before moving to England. Later she returned to Ireland, where she is now an advocate for other survivors.

Girl in the
Tunnel

My Story of Love and Loss as a
Survivor of the Magdalene Laundries

MAUREEN SULLIVAN

MERRION
PRESS

First published in 2023 by

Merrion Press

10 George's Street

Newbridge

Co. Kildare

Ireland

www.merrionpress.ie

978 1 78537 452 4 (Paper)

978 1 78537 451 7 (Ebook)

A CIP catalogue record for this book is
available from the British Library.

Typeset in Calluna 12/17 pt

Cover design by Fiachra McCarthy

Merrion Press is a member of Publishing Ireland.

This book is dedicated to my daughter, Michelle, my son, Jamie, and my grandchild, Lauryn.

CONTENTS

AUTHOR'S NOTE

This is the story of what happened to me nearly sixty years ago, when I confided in a teacher about the abuse I was suffering at home. What followed led me to lose my voice completely and I did not speak of it until much later in my life. But it is a story that should be told, no matter what.

It might surprise you, or it might not, to know that there are people still pushing me to stay silent. There are people who want this book kept from your hands. People who say to me in the street, 'Would you not get over it?' People who tell me to shut up about it – they defend men and they defend the Catholic Church.

But this is my story to tell and this is how I remember it. I've told it as best I can.

I changed most of the names in this book – my abuser, relatives, locals and the nuns – because I'm not out to hurt or for revenge. I wrote this book because I was silenced as a child when I was a victim of abuse and I was silenced by society when I left the laundry. I want people to know what happened. This is my history, but it's also the history of this country.

What I have told you here – all of it – is absolutely true.

If you don't think I should speak up, if you think this is the wrong thing to do, that's your opinion. What you think of me is none of my business. But I want this story told before I leave this world.

So I am sharing my story, telling you my secrets, so I can finally walk free from all of it.

Maureen Sullivan

PROLOGUE

I never knew my father, John L. Sullivan, but there was a photograph of him on the wall in my grandmother's house. As a child my granny would lift me up to see this young man in black and white, his collar open and his hair combed, smiling as he stood for his photo at the crossroads beyond in Bennekerry.

'This is your father,' my granny would say. 'Don't ever forget it.'

In Carlow, at that time, photographs were not common, certainly not in the poorest of houses – like ours was – and so I feel lucky to have seen his face at all.

My older brother, Michael, is the only one with memories of him, but they are fleeting, nothing more than a shadow leaning over his cot.

My mother was nineteen and pregnant with me when my father died suddenly. Michael was two and my other brother, Paddy, was only eight months. They all lived with my granny in her tiny two-storey cottage in the middle of the Irish countryside. That was where I was born a few months later, in the little parlour off the main room – the same room that my newly-wed parents had first slept in together.

After my father died that room was left empty, except for a small table in the corner on which his billhook lay.

**

Granny told us that my father was out riding one day and got caught in the rain. A few days later he fell gravely ill. He died three days after that. That's how the story was told to me anyway. I feel really sad, a truly great and deep sorrow, when I think about my young mother at his bedside, with him slipping away so fast, and then at his graveside with a toddler, a baby in her arms and another on the way.

After he was gone she never mentioned him again.

Perhaps it was fear, perhaps disappointment, that silenced his name in her mouth. Disappointment for the life she had planned with my father, for the home they were to make together. Fear of being a widow in Ireland, with three babies to feed and no husband to support them. In those days widows could not turn to the government for support, and any pension that was available was a pittance, especially for women whose late husbands had dug ditches and cut back hedgerows for a few pence a week. My mother was left destitute, as far as I know anyway. That is how it was.

Granny was very poor, living in a little house that had no electricity or running water, and although she loved us very much, she could not support us. I imagine the reason my mother rushed to marry Marty Murphy, a gammy-footed pig dealer from Carlow town, was to save us from starvation.

Some think I was lucky to escape the hardship of losing my father, saying to me that it was, in ways, a blessing that I was born later and never felt the loss, but I feel it deeply in my own way. Maybe I would have felt better if I'd known him, but I was just left to wonder if he would have loved me. What would he have called me? Would I have had a special name from him only?

Would he have come to find me when they took me away? Would he have broken down the doors to steal me back home?

Inside I really grieve for what I never had. I grieve for the man in the photograph, the smiling, curly-headed young man who I have spent my life longing for. I grieve for the happy home he had with my mother, the love and laughter that was there, and the childhood I lost when he died. I think of what my life would have been, if only John L. Sullivan had never taken his horse out on a cold, wet day.

Nobody ever spoke about my father except Granny, who told me he was a kind and gentle person. Is it possible to miss something you never had? It feels like it. Even now, the child that's left in me calls out for her father in the dark and cries when he doesn't come. If my father hadn't gone out that day, and hadn't caught a chill that led to such a serious illness that he didn't survive, I would have had a childhood where my parents' love for one another surrounded me and my brothers too. I think often about fate and how the event of his death changed the path of my whole life, even before I was born. When I was on the way, safe in my mother's womb, I was a child of a loving marriage, with two parents planning a future for me, one of happiness and warmth.

But that was not meant to be.

Instead, I was born into a life where my family was displaced, where my father was dead and unable to protect me, where I was placed in the care of monsters and stolen away to be neglected, abused and abandoned to evil.

1

MARTY

I told on him, didn't I? That was the crime. That's what happened. I told the Church that my stepfather was molesting and raping me, and beating me and my brothers.

So they punished me for it.

I still lie in bed trying to figure it out, what I did and why was I sent away to a prison to work as a slave? What was my crime?

It's simple. I told on *him*. I told on Marty.

***

Before I was two my mother married that lame pig jobber from Green Lane in Carlow town called Marty Murphy. He is, I suppose, the only father I ever knew. He hurt me the day I was carried into his house, with a hard slap to my legs, and he hurts me still today, though he has been dead for years. The mental, physical and sexual torture I suffered in my childhood, that can never be erased or settled. I live with it.

5

I am a product of it.

***

I don't know if you know Carlow, but Green Lane runs up through it, near the cathedral. Marty's house was two old cottages knocked together, just past the crossroads at the school there. Our house was attached to another cottage, where his brother Shay lived. Shay was a nice man. He always had a smile for us when we passed by him, or a pat on the head or the shoulder where his hand would rest for a minute and pass a bit of energy to you, in the way good people do. Even better than that, from my point of view anyway, every now and again he would beat Marty up, if he saw a bruise or bleeding lip on me or my brothers. They would fall out over all sorts of things, but most often over how Marty treated us children, and Shay would wail on Marty shouting, 'Leave them alone, you bastard,' as he boxed lumps out of him. They would roll around on the mud floor, or in the dust of the yard, boxing each other and pinning, or being pinned, until they ran out of steam and stopped, bloodied and exhausted. Then they wouldn't speak for weeks. I loved the fights, seeing Marty knocked senseless, but the aftermath for me and my brothers was never worth it.

Marty hated us. There is no other way to explain it. We were called 'Sullivan bastards'. We had no other names in that house. He called us that when he wanted us and when he referred to us. Looking back, with my adult mind, I know he was like a little dog that bites because it is scared of everything. Maybe he was scared of losing my mother, scared of not having con-trol over the world around him ... or maybe he was jealous, in

6

some twisted way, of my father and the real love my mother had before she met Marty; he was second in line after all. And I am sure he knew my father. Maybe we reminded him of that. God knows, and who cares? Those things are explanations, not excuses. Marty Murphy was twisted and that is that.

We lived near Carlow cathedral. It's an ornate grey stone building, in the way most cathedrals are, designed to evoke fear. Marty made a beeline for that place every single day, like most Irish men did back then, to catch ten o'clock Mass with the bishop. He was first in and last out, always making sure to be seen, limping in and out like a martyr. We always said the Rosary at night in his house too.

In the cottage there was a tin bath, like you see in old movies, where one end slopes up for you to rest your back. My mother would boil and fill, boil and fill with water heated on our old cooker. It was back-breaking work, work she would stand against the table to recover from as Marty lowered himself into the hot water. He always bathed first and took his time, then my mother would get in and out quickly, and one by one the children would be washed. The Sullivan bastards were last.

By the time it was my turn to get into the water, it would be cold, and grey from the dust, dirt and skin of the others; swirling hairs from the adults' bodies would float in it and stick to my skin. When I could get away with it, I'd get halfway in and then straight out.

The floors in Green Lane were clay and sawdust, like most of the poor homes around us. The sawdust was there to soak up the Irish rain that came so often, and the spilled tea or bathwater that splashed out. Every now and again Marty and Shay would take up the floor coverings, digging out the old sawdust and clay to replace them with new. The smell of sour and must would be gone for a while when they did that.

Ireland was a different place then. Being poor meant you suffered physically, from cold and hunger. We survived mostly on bread, and it was hard Irish bread that you don't see these days. It was kept in a large tin beside the cooker. We would sometimes soften it with water or dip it into tea. Food was kept in the 'larder', which was a large press, but there was rarely anything in it. Milk was kept in cans that we refilled at the shop in the town and we sometimes had Stork margarine to use as butter. We never had real butter. We had eggs from Granny's chickens.

In those days not much thought was given over to nutrition, certainly not of common children anyway. Not like it is today. The Sullivan children sat on orange boxes at a nailed-together table made from an old door or – as more and more children came along – stood for our meals. Some of the time we ate with our hands – there was never enough cutlery for everyone. If we were lucky, we would have scraps of meat from a pig's head with its eyes still in that my mother boiled up on Sunday, but the Murphys ate first, so oftentimes we got nothing. We were seen as cuckoos. If there was no meat, we would have an Oxo cube or Chef's Sauce spread on wetted bread, with whatever few vegetables we had.

There was never enough.

Marty, however, never went without. He was fed first and always had a supply of his two great loves, Erinmore tobacco and Irel coffee, which came in a bottle and was stirred into hot water. He took it with milk. Not having any milk when Marty wanted coffee was a sentence for punishment, so myself and my brothers pre-empted this and other things we would get in trouble for by taking preventative action. It's something I still struggle with today, as I find myself fretting if I run out of milk, even though I'm the only one here.

In those days you went for milk with a small can on a wire. Ours was, like most, made of tin, I think, with a wire looped around it that was so thin it would cut your fingers when the can was full and heavy with milk. There were no milk cartons stacked up in fridges in shops like there are now, just big milk churns out the backs of shops from which the shopkeeper would fill your can. That was the norm back then.

Like most people in those days, we had an outhouse with our cottage, just your basic privy with no flush. Scraps of paper hung on a nail, which was also the norm in Irish houses at the time, that we had cut up from newspapers we found around the town. We could never have bought one. We barely had enough money to live.

That privy was dug out when it was full. On hot days the smell of it would stick in your throat and make you retch, and you would be swarmed with flies when you went into it. At night the family used a bucket to save going out into the dark.

Young people these days don't know the luxury they live in. I don't think they can fathom it. Only fifty or sixty years ago they would have had to carry a bucket of urine down to empty it in the morning, like I had to when I was too small to take the weight of it and so it would slop out all over my feet. As I had no fresh clothes, just one or two things I could wear, I stank of wee all day – my socks were always yellow and stinking from it and I knew it and I was embarrassed. I used to long for the clean white socks that the farmers' daughters wore to school. I would hide my feet under my chair and dream of new socks.

***

My brothers and I were terrified of Marty Murphy from day one. He didn't restrain himself and lost his temper in a second, sometimes for nothing you could place, and he would go for you, even in his boots, and his kicks would hurt for days. His flying hands, thumping closed fists would have you seeing stars. He really hated us. Or he hated himself, maybe, for what he couldn't stop doing to us, but either way living with Marty was like living with the devil himself. We suffered every single day.

We all slept in beds together. In Green Lane there were two rooms, with two double beds in each one. My mother and Marty were in the front room in a bed with a baby, across from a bed with the youngest ones. In the other room there was me, my brothers and the others. We didn't have duvets or even blankets most of the time. It was coats on top of us and we would sleep close for the heat of each other to get through the night.

Sometimes we might fight, a small shift would pull a coat off someone's leg or shoulder and they'd resist or pull back, and there'd end up being a tussle for warmth. The door would whack open, hitting the wall like the wind whipped it, and Marty Murphy would cross the floor to where me and my brothers lay and stop any fighting – even if we weren't involved – with a box to our bodies or faces. If he was thumping me, I'd deal with it by rolling away or covering my head so that he would land that cruel hand on my back or shoulders. But if he went for my brothers, I would be so afraid I would sometimes wet myself.

Hearing that snarl as he drew back his fists to land them on the bodies of the people I loved was harder than taking it myself. I'd feel the warmth of spreading urine under me and be upset and shocked that it had happened and terrified that one of the others would notice and I'd be battered too.

Marty frightened me in a different way than he frightened my brothers. They were always on their guard for punches and kicks, they watched out for flashes of anger to cross his face so they could run. I watched out for a different look eventually – a curl of his lip and a way of fixing his eyes on me that I would learn to be terrified of. From a young age I was on my guard for something more sinister. Something so violent the wounds have never healed.

Something I didn't understand at all.

2

GRANNY

About an hour's walk from Green Lane is the small village of Bennekerry, where my father's people were all from, and where my brother still lives in my granny's cottage, on a bend in the road near the river.

My earliest memory is there, when I, aged less than two, fell backwards into the basin of boiling water that Granny had drained from a pot of potatoes. She never wasted hot water and would use this to wash shirts. My back was scalded. I remember that, just that moment as a single memory, and then I remember my granny applying cream she had made from herbs and earth to the burns, and some relief from that. I remember, though, that I cried with the pain when she applied it and that made Granny cry too, and we sat together for a while in a harmony of wails.

To get to Granny's you went through two standing stones that opened the hedgerows and exposed a small two-storey cottage, with rooms in the attic and a huge hearth right in the middle. It was tiny and tumbledown and leaked rain in places, but to me it was a sanctuary from everything that was going on at home. It was a place where everything was warm, where everything was good and I was not hurt or afraid.

It was dark inside, with the thickest walls you can imagine, so thick that when I was little, I could stand in the doorway and my shoulders wouldn't be as wide as the wall. It had sand-on-screed floors and oil lamps that were lit in the late afternoon, and a window set into the thick wall that barely let light in, except when the sun was low – then it flooded the downstairs like a tomb. I remember the smell of the oil lamps, like sulphur.

There was a fire in the sitting room, a table with three chairs and an Irish dresser that – as Irish dressers at that time tended to – held every item or knick-knack that Granny owned. It wasn't much. The walls were whitewashed for light, the wash painted straight onto the stones the cottage was built from.

On the wall there she hung her best dress on a nail, replaced by her everyday clothes on Sundays – once they were washed – and her coat on another nail by the door. Granny wore long clothes, a skirt made of wool to her ankles and a blouse under a knitted jumper. She always had an apron on, in the pocket of which she kept things in the way another woman might use a handbag. In this pocket was her money, her pipe and bits and bobs. I loved the sound it made when her hands went into it. I loved the way she would pull it open and cast an eye over the contents, or root around in there for whatever it was she wanted.

She was old IRA, my grandmother. Carlow had a lot of action in those times of the 1910s and '20s, and Irish women did their bit. Granny certainly did; she fought alongside her brothers against the Black and Tans during the War of Independence.

Granny lived with her brother Jack, who we called Grandad or Uncle Jack depending on the day. He was a quiet, kind man who made his few bob cutting hedges and digging ditches, like my own father had, for local farmers. Jack's hands told that story – brown and creased and scratched – and I loved to watch him pack his pipe. The rhythm and the small sounds his movements made, the scrapes and soft tapping sounds as he pressed the tobacco into the bowl with care, would leave me entranced and drowsy. The smell of tobacco in fresh air still reminds me of Jack and the good feelings that would come with that smell, because he only smoked on Sundays and that meant we would have meat for dinner and butter on our potatoes. It was a different smell to the cheap tobacco I was used to at home, smoked all the time and left go stale in its pouch. That was sour.

The walk to Bennekerry from our house was long, but we never thought about that. How else would you get there? It probably took an hour each way. But in those days people walked, and time was different. We didn't think about it in the same way people do now. We just got on with it. Granny didn't have a watch, but she was never late for us, she would use other things to tell time – what way the sun looked in the sky, what the birds were doing, or who she saw pass on the road that told her it was time to go for us. When we saw her at the gate, we never thought about the time it was going to take us to get to her house. It was the routine. Everybody walked everywhere. There were no cars bombing around the back roads the way there are now. You didn't really know people with a car, but if you did see one about to pass, oftentimes you'd flag it down and take a lift. That was exciting as a child, but it didn't matter either way, our legs were young. Granny was used to the walk, but sometimes she would stop and give herself a breather, to maybe take a drink of water from the pumps that stood on the side of the road. We would pass people she knew and she might stop and talk for a minute, or go into Sharkey's shop for something she needed. In the winter, by the time we reached her cottage it would be getting dark and cold, and we would be welcomed by the fire in the hearth in her tiny kitchen that had been lit first thing and kept going during the day as best she could. Arriving in to that warmth with cold fingers, knees and noses, the three of us kids would crowd around the fire, and stand there almost hypnotised until we warmed up. Granny would begin getting some dinner on, sending us this way and that to help.

**

There was a donkey at Granny's house. A big old Irish donkey with a name I don't remember, who stood at the gate into Granny's field. His nose was like velvet and his breath came out in big breathy *hmph*s. Whenever he saw us coming back from school at the weekend, he would start up braying like his life was over, and Granny would cluck at him as she passed, rubbing his nose and pulling the last of a cut-up apple from her apron pocket.

'Will you whist,' she would say to him, 'you big eejit,' but she would kiss him on the nose sometimes if she thought nobody was looking. There were also always two pigs in a shed up around the back of her cottage. Everyone kept pigs who had room.

At night Granny would herd us, clucking and promising stories, into her soft bed. The mattress was so old it hung like a hammock between the iron sides and she held us against her as she slept, all three of us. She had a child on each side, under her arm, and the last one in would sleep along her soft old body with their head on her chest. To fall asleep there was the goal of each of us, and so we would fight for that spot. Granny's house was the opposite to home, where the only touch we felt was in anger and hurt. We recharged in Granny's arms. We felt the energy of her love.

There was no pub in Bennekerry, but even if there had been, in those days women weren't served at the bar, if at all. My granny always had a baby of Powers whiskey by her bed. Just before she would lie down to sleep, with all of us already clinging to her, she would take a teaspoon of it. She said it was good for her blood.

***

Granny was a radical. She never married, but she had three children. Two of them were removed from her by the state and one she managed to keep hold of – my father. She was, for all intents and purposes, although she didn't name it, a natural-born feminist, known for speaking her mind and taking no crap from the parish priest, who tried – unsuccessfully – to marry her off to local men a few times. On one occasion, at the altar, opposite a quiet man named James Roche, she asked if she would have to give up her own house and the priest said she would, telling her that her duty as a wife would be to live with her husband and care for him. The story goes that she was pregnant at the time, and apparently she said, 'Well I'm not marrying then,' and walked off out of the church.

James Roche was so bewitched by my grandmother that he never married anyone else and would visit her at her gate for the rest of her life. It is presumed all of her children were his. So he was my grandfather. I remember him so well, hearing his voice call out my granny's name – 'Katie' – as he leaned a shoulder onto the gate posts and rooted in the pocket of his tweed jacket for sweets for us, his grandchildren. I wish we had known. We just called him 'Old James' and raced to see him when he called, but we never considered our real relationship until we were older.

In the winter the three-mile walk from Green Lane to Granny's house felt five times longer. The wind in Carlow, because it is so flat there, carries over the ground so fast it whipped against our bare legs as we walked down the winding roads. You'd hear the sound of it, like banshees, as the evenings turned dark. Children in those days wore skirts or shorts, our legs left open to the elements, because material was expensive and children were – unimaginably – dispensable. But we didn't mind it, not on Fridays anyway, when we would walk from school to Granny's cottage with joy and freedom to distract us from the weather, and sure we would arrive with chattering teeth and shoulders shaking but delighted to be in her warm cottage with its hot food and roaring fire. Our hands would be so cold we wouldn't be able to undo our buttons and once we got inside the door we would huddle around the fire, almost getting into it, to warm up. Granny would start the ritual of tea-making, and unwrap slices of Chester cake that she had stopped at Sharkey's shop for. You see, Friday was her pension day and she always made room in her tiny budget for the delicious pressed cake made from odds and ends from the bakery. With Chester cake you never knew what you would get – a raisin or a piece of chocolate or cherry was like winning the lottery. You can still get Chester cake these days, but it doesn't taste the same; you need a starving tummy to really enjoy it to the full.

Tea is sacred to most Irish people and in Granny's cottage it was a serious thing. Her tea was kept in a can and it was stirred carefully into boiling water. She knew the right moment to take the kettle off the fire to make sure to scald the leaves. And she had patience with that, knowing that too soon would ruin a good cup of tea, no matter how thirsty we were for it. Her recipe was one spoon per person and 'one for the pot'. I still make pots of tea the same way, although, of course, instead of spoons I use bags now. My granny always poured the hot, dark tea in on top of milk and sugar, and we warmed ourselves with it.

When Granny served us tea, she would always say the same thing, 'Don't drop your cup.' We were sure, at the time, that meant her cups were expensive, but thinking back they were simple enamel, the ones with the blue stripe. I know now that a dent in them could cause rust and rust could make us sick, so she was careful with them and careful with us. We always washed them extra carefully, in the barrel at the back of the house where rainwater collected. We never drank that water; drinking water was taken from the village well in buckets every day and kept in the kitchen.

I remember my brother's face one day when he saw Granny empty out her chamber pot into the ditch and then, just before she brought it back in she dipped it into the rain barrel where we washed our cups. He was astonished.

'Granny that's where we wash our cups,' he said, but Granny just laughed and said, 'Isn't it the best tea you've ever had?' As if that was the secret to it.

Granny lived how she lived and would be just as astonished to see how we live now, I feel. I think of her all the time, when I turn on a tap, or switch my heating on. I think of her carrying pails of water along the road, or building a fire and working to keep it going as hard as she had to, or making feasts from scraps to make some joy in the lives of the children she loved.

Granny noticed our bruises. She would look at them and dress the bad ones with herbs and tinctures she bought from a healing woman up the hill, but she never spoke of our life at Marty's with us. But it seemed she loved us extra hard when we were hurt, held us on her knee and coaxed us into little kisses, telling us we were good and kind children and to never let any-one make us believe something else. She gave us that love to balance out the brutality, fuelled us with it to get us through the week. I believe she thought she would lose all contact with us if she rocked the boat. Don't forget, she knew the power the Church had over children more than most. She had her own babies taken away after all. She was not my mother's mother, or Marty's, and so had no rights or influence over what happened to us.

So she mumbled curses under her breath when we were badly hurt, and healed us with her potions and her heart when she could. At our worst times she would take down the photo of our father from the wall and show it to us. We would hang off her shoulder, as she sat in her chair, to look at it and she would go through his story, and ours, again and again.

'This man, this man here in this photo, is your father.'

She told us stories of how he was a champion boxer and a military man. She would trace her finger gently across his smiling face and sigh and take a moment.

A real fine man, she would say. Strong, she would say. One blow from John Sullivan would land a regular man flat on his back, she would say. I dribbled over those stories. I used to imagine my father rearing up to hit Marty Murphy a puck in the mouth. I wished and wished that would happen.

One time my brothers and I heard her mutter, 'He was barely cold in that grave,' as she hung the photo back on its nail. I know now what she meant – she was disappointed with my mother's choices – but I didn't know then. We talked about it all the way to school on the following Monday and came to the conclusion he must have died in winter. We thought maybe she put blankets in the coffin.

When Granny came to visit it was brief, small stops in to check we were all alive, I think. And when she was in Green Lane, she behaved herself. In those days men had full control of the family, much more than they do now, and wives had no rights. My granny knew that it was up to Marty if she saw us, so she played the game. But she saw the contrast between us Sullivans and my mother's second family. She saw that his children had fat on their chins while we were gaunt; we were neglected and covered in bruises, while they were playing and happy. Granny never spoke directly to Marty, she channelled conversations with him through my mother or gave him clipped responses and dagger eyes.

⁂

Our granny was on our side. Her home was poorer than ours, but she fed us with love and shared what she had with us. She stretched everything into a feast, made everything exciting. She had a pit where potatoes and onions were kept in the dark – they lasted longer that way and didn't sprout or go green. It felt endless and she would say, 'Ah *alanna*, there isn't a potato inside in that pit, but sure go look anyway,' and we would run out to see if we could find something and there was always some there. Like loaves and fishes, there was always enough. She was a magic maker.

Granny would sometimes send us to the field down the way to get some vegetables, whatever was growing. It was a field belonging, of course, to a farmer, and so for all intents and purposes we were pilfering. But we never saw it like that, and to be honest I still don't now. There is no crime or sin in feeding starving children.

Usually that farmer grew turnips, or carrots, one year on, one year off, and we always only took one turnip or four carrots from the corner anyway, where they grew small or out of shape. You played the lottery even so, learning that you can never judge the size of a vegetable from the size of the leaves above the ground.

I don't know if you've ever pulled a turnip, but it takes some effort when you are three foot and weigh nothing. I used to fall backwards with the momentum once the root gave way from the ground. More times than one I would be destroyed with the muck by the time I got my prize. The soil that Irish farmers grow root vegetables in is as thick as cement.

There'd be a cheer from my brothers if the turnip we pulled was a good one. Chuffed, the looter would carry it like a baby all the way back to Granny and feel great pride as it was boiled up for our dinner.

One meal Granny used to make for us was 'goody' – hard, stale bread pulled apart into pieces and put into a cup and then softened with hot water. Then you sprinkle it with white sugar and pour milk over it. A poor man's bread pudding. I loved it and it was my absolute favourite thing to eat. I would give anything to eat it again, but Irish bread is so soft and fresh these days it just wouldn't be the same, so I just think about it instead. It's a lovely memory.

The anticipation while Granny would be making the goody is yet unmatched in my life for the excitement. We would be hopping. When she served it, we would slow to a snail's pace, not one of us wanting to be the first to finish – we wanted to make it last. Our little heels would be swinging or banging on the floor with gusto for the sugar and the real enjoyment of the treat.

**

Granny often sent us to collect 'cipíns' along the ditch by her house, which were small twists of sticks that fell from the trees overnight and that made perfect kindling for the fire. She was always on the lookout for them, collected them all the time. I roll the memory of those hunts over in my mind when I am tired and need comfort – the feeling of my granny's hand on my chest, the way she would check the buttons of our coats were holding, the little pat and push out the door with instructions, her trust in me to find good ones.

She watched us from the window as we ran down into the field to where the trees were, her shawl folded through her arms that she held across her chest. We bent and collected, and she called out encouragement. When our hands were full, or when the light dimmed – whichever was first – she would call us back and her warm words were enough reward for the job.

When I look back now through my memories and ask myself what happiness I might have known as a child, my head is filled with the face of my granny. My heart longs for that tiny cottage and the little soft woman who made the hours there so filled with love and light they carried me through what was to come.

I often lean down to lift small sticks when I see them and walk along for a while with a small bundle in my hand, cherishing the memory of my granny and wishing I could see her again.

3

MY MOTHER

My mother was lovely looking when she was young. She was a match for my good-looking father – I can see it in the photos we have of her, with dark curly hair framing large blue eyes and high cheekbones. Granny said she used to take care of herself when she was being courted by my father, but after he died, she stopped. She never wore make-up ever or fixed her hair ever again, no matter what.

She said to me when I asked that she never had the money or the time for it. She had thirteen children and a husband to appease and it seemed like she had lived a thousand years before she was forty.

My mother was always working, either at home, when she was on her feet without a break from dusk till dawn, or at one of the two jobs she had to bring money in, at the pub, the local B&B and later, in the Sacred Heart care home.

I remember she was at Marty's beck and call, even though, in my memory, she did more to bring money into our home than he ever did. She was always working, while he just sat there sucking his pipe, interrupting her to look for a cup of coffee. He always blew smoke out through his dirty teeth just before he would call her name. That pause never failed to catch her attention and she would stop and turn when he said, 'Mary.' He spoke to her like she was paid staff, rolling his shoulders back into the comfort of his chair while she sat peeling spuds on a broken stool.

Who decided that anyway? That all women are good for is to serve men? When did that start? If my mother had sat down in that chair and ordered coffee from her husband, even once, she would probably have been sent to an asylum. And not as much has changed there as we like to pretend. Women come second and do everything, even in these modern times.

It's not fair.

Marty bred my mother until she was wore out and humbled to nothing but a 'mammy'. She had no interests, no hobbies and she never got anything from him, not even a card on her birthday, not that I ever saw.

I never saw Marty hit my mother. But whatever power he had over her, he used it. She simply wasn't allowed to *love* her first three, the bastards, and that was how it was. She wasn't allowed.

When I think about what I was put through, and what my brothers were put through, in that house, I have to ask myself what my mother was going through to put up with it. Was she that broken? Or was she stamped so far into the ground she could only eat the dirt? Was she so destroyed in her second marriage by that brute, or – and this is something I think about a lot – did she suffer the same in her childhood as I did in mine?

My mother's mother mentioned once, when I was in the room to overhear, that my mother would often be tore out of bed in the evenings by her bad-tempered father to go fetch him a bottle of stout from the pub. It doesn't take a genius to figure out that there was a problem in that home for sure. And also from the way she was so passive about the horrors her children suffered – the beatings alone would have had most mothers baring teeth, but not mine. She turned a blind eye and got on with it.

It used to make me so frustrated before I knew how things were for Irish women. I'd ask myself, why didn't my mother run away to Granny's with all of us? I wished she would. Granny always had enough potatoes in that pit. She was magical. She could have fed all of us. I was sure love alone could have fed all of my mother's children, if only my mother would run away. Of course, I didn't understand anything. As I got older, I wanted to know why she didn't stop him or leave him, if not for me, for herself? I'm over those questions now.

It's hard to imagine the reasons for people behaving as they did, given how fast Ireland has progressed, and it's hard to imagine how my mother thought things through. I know now she had no choices – women were the property of their husbands. Their bodies belonged to the men they married, their children did too. Mary Quinn was the property of Marty Murphy. She was his wife and if even the parish priest – with all his power – did not use it to stop Marty from abusing children, what could my mother have done? Left him? Did you know, in Ireland back then that custody of children was with the husbands? My mother would have had to leave her children, even us, with Marty. She would have been seen as a disgrace and may not have seen us again.

I remember one day my granny was chatting to a neighbour up at our house and she said something that my mother misunderstood when she overheard it, and she thought my granny was telling on Marty. She flew back into the house and grabbed me and hissed, 'What is Granny saying out there? What did you tell Granny, Maureen?'

I said, 'I didn't tell anything, she isn't saying anything,' and she let me go and stood against the open window, listening.

Then she grabbed me again. 'Are you sure, Maureen? Did Michael or Paddy maybe say something?' She kept flicking her eyes to mine, then back to the window.

I nodded, swore I'd said nothing. I didn't even know what she thought I said, but I denied it. She pushed me on it and I told the truth. I had said nothing.

Ireland was never a country for women. The Church reigned supreme and women kept a low profile. There was punishment for speaking up against the system, against the way they wanted it kept – any act that made Ireland look less than perfect to the Church in Rome was punished severely. That's why women were disappeared back then. That's why I was.

I believe my mother kept any soul she had dormant and suppressed her feelings. Any dreams she had had for her life, well, she buried them with my father, her true love. She survived as best she could. I try to understand her. She did her best with the position she was in, as a woman in Ireland in the 1950s and '60s. Just because I think I would do things differently doesn't mean I know, because I cannot really understand her at all. I don't want to look down on her, and I don't. She was who she was and I loved her very much, even with all of what happened. When she was dying of a stroke in Sacred Heart, where she had worked all her life, I went there every day to give her her dinner. I spooned the food into her with love, and then I helped her lie down to sleep for the night, kissed her cheek and told her I loved her. I have no regrets about my relationship with my mother. Nobody knows what she went through in her life, so nobody should judge her.

My mother eventually did leave Marty. When we were all grown up, she packed a bag and walked out without a word. She rang me in London, where I was living. I had written to her with the number for the phone box near my flat, and we had arranged by letter a time when she would call me once a week. I used to wait by the box, worrying someone would use it before it rang for me.

When I answered it this time, I could hear she was excited. Her voice was raised and fast.

'Well, I left him, Maureen,' she said, 'I left Marty.'

That was all that was really said on the phone. I said I was happy for her and I'll admit I cried. She did too.

'Will you come back, Maureen?' she said. She always asked me that.

'I don't know, Mam,' I said.

Then the ten pence ran out and we were warned to top up or lose the call, so we said goodbye instead.

I didn't see her for a good while after that.

4

ABUSE

Marty Murphy abused me. From the day I toddled into his house I was beaten. But later, when I was older, he sexually assaulted me. Sometimes every day for a few weeks, then maybe there would be weeks between it at other times.

I was eight the first time. He caught me inside the door of their bedroom when my mother was at work and I was minding the smallest. I'd just put that baby down when he appeared in the doorway of their room. Something was off with him. He put his hand on my shoulder in a way he never had before and told me he had something he needed to explain to me, because I needed to know it. Marty had never touched me kindly, but instead of being glad of it, my guard went up and I flinched. I knew something terrible was happening, I could tell by the way he was moving and the way he spoke in almost a whisper. My intuition told me this was bad.

Marty explained to me, leaning over me so I could feel his breath on the top of my head, that men need to be milked like cattle and said I had to do it. He let his braces off his shoulders and pushed his trousers down a bit and showed me what he wanted me to do. I was so full of fear, it felt as though my body was burning. I shook my head, but he said I had to do it or I'd have to stay home and not go to Granny's. I resisted anyway and so he boxed me across the face and told me to do it. So I did. I did what he showed me, to avoid a beating, to avoid the threats he continued to whisper, and he showed me the milk that came out of him. It covered my wrist and arm. I didn't want to do it, but he made me over and over again, night after night when my mother was at work. And later he did worse. I was warned not to make a sound or he would kill me. I believed it and I bore it all. The sexual molestation and eventually the rapes that would leave me with pains in my hips and abdomen, and cramping that would sometimes make me vomit. I was often so sore that moving my legs was agony and I could only shuffle to school miles behind the others. I got scolded every day for lateness.

You can understand now why Fridays meant so much to me and why I ran to my lovely granny and clung to her like I was drowning. We all did, the three of us. On Fridays, when we would walk to her cottage three miles away instead of down the road home, we would often break into a run when we saw her at the school gate and she would sweep us into her arms and kiss the tops of our heads one by one with soft chucks and whistles, like a mother hen. We fought to hold her hands, three hands fighting for two. If I was sore and couldn't run, the boys would get there first and take her hands and when I would catch up, I would grab a fistful of her coat and hold that all the way home.

Marty knew what those weekends meant to us. He knew that our time with Granny was precious and he used that against us. There were constant hints that he might happen to need us around at the weekend, made suddenly if we didn't move fast enough to do his bidding. Or sometimes he was more blatant about it and would outright threaten to keep me at home if I so much as resisted the things he did to me. And often he would actually stop me going, keeping me at home for the weekend as my brothers went off. Just because he could.

Those moments, when I'd see her at the gate and I'd raise my hand and shake my head and turn left instead of into her embrace, those were the lowest moments of my childhood. Knowing what I was going home to be used for, knowing that my brothers would be free of it all and I wouldn't, not for another week at least, was torture.

My mother had a baby almost every year and the times that she spent in hospital were times I would never see Granny at all. At those times we would see our other granny, my mother's mother. She was a tall, cold woman who didn't mind – and seemed to almost enjoy – getting us in trouble. In fact she would often land us in it. Once, when my mother was in hospital having a baby and her mother was minding us, she asked me to bounce the pram, which I did for an hour. Those prams were set onto huge springs and the baby would be almost out of it sometimes if you bounced them too hard. It was a boring job and on that day I spotted my other granny, my real one, passing through the crossroads. I knew where she was going – up to sow potatoes in the fields above. The baby was asleep, so I left the pram outside the door – there was no harm in that in them days – and ran after her.

'*Alanna*,' she said when I caught up with her, 'are you alright to be coming with me?'

I nodded. I wasn't going to lie, but I was giving myself permission.

Up in the fields the air was that crisp cool air you get around St Patrick's Day, the kind of air the sun won't take long to warm up if the clouds pass. That day they did, just as we got to the field and Granny took our coats and laid them over the gate. Then the two of us made our way to the farmer to let him know we could work. There were other people doing the job as well, all arranged by word of mouth and tradition, in the way things were in those days.

Potatoes don't have seeds, they grow from each other.

'Same way people do,' Granny said with a wink, but the joke went over my head.

In huge bags were halved and quartered potatoes, and those were pushed into rows made in advance and covered up with soil, by hand.

Bending used to hurt Granny if she did it too much, so I helped her do the covering up, patting the soil back over the potato that was pushed into the ground.

When her bag was empty, she was done, and the farmer gave her a penny.

We walked back through the crossroads together, and she went straight for Bennekerry and I ran as fast as I could back to our house again.

Granny Quinn was at the door, with a crying baby in her arms.

'You little bitch!' she roared, catching me by the collar and dragging me into the house.

'I'm sorry, Granny,' I said, but I had no excuse prepared, 'I was with Granny in the field for the potatoes.'

'Did I say you could go do that?' Her eyes were furious. 'Wait till Marty gets back!'

I was so horrified I almost wet myself. 'No, no, Granny Quinn, don't tell Marty, please.'

I remember wishing I'd never gone. He was going to murder me stone dead. I knew it.

Marty came home about an hour later from the beet factory where he did casual work, dressed in a white smock. I heard Granny Quinn tell him that I had left the baby outside and run off to play in the fields with 'that old witch', which is what she called my beautiful granny. Then she left.

Needless to say I got a terrible beating.

Granny Quinn made another appearance at our house that same night. She had gone to see my mother in hospital, who had asked her to bring me down.

Granny Quinn didn't seem to notice much as I left with her. I kept my head down and of course I hadn't seen myself. Halfway to the hospital she suddenly gasped and said, 'What happened your face?'

I touched it. I didn't know what I looked like.

'Jesus, girl, did Marty do that?' she said and took a compact mirror out of her bag and showed me the state Marty had left me in. I had a huge purple bruise spreading over my jaw and cheekbone. And my eye was blood red.

'He did because I went up with Granny,' I said, and she rolled her eyes.

'Well,' she said, 'I suppose that's what you get.'

'You told on me,' I narrowed my eyes.

'Well, you won't do it again, will you?' she said.

When we went into the hospital and up the stairs to where the ward of mothers and babies was, the nurse on duty let out a gasp and said, 'What happened to the child?'

'Ah,' my grandmother said, 'she is a little tomboy this one.'

When we saw my mother, my grandmother said, 'There was trouble with him,' and my mother said nothing to me about it.

The baby looked like all the other ones.

***

Another time Granny Quinn sent me out to mind the youngest ones, and I pushed the pram up Green Lane to the graveyard where we joined a funeral. It was something to do and I liked the air up there. The babies were asleep, head to toe in the pram, and I listened to the prayers and watched the men lower the coffin into the grave, and when that was done, I stood there for a minute thinking about my own father in his grave up at the church in Bennekerry, before I walked the pram back to the house.

When I got there Granny Quinn was at the door and she flew at me, 'Where were you, you little bitch?' she said. 'I told you to walk the babies, not disappear for hours with them.'

I said, 'I was watching a funeral, Granny. They're asleep.'

And she reefed the pram from me and pushed me into the house.

When Marty got back she told on me again, just before she left, standing in the open door.

'That one,' she said, and pointed at me, 'was missing for two hours today and says she was at a funeral. Have you ever heard the like?'

'A funeral?' he asked, and he cocked his head and narrowed his eyes. 'It's only Protestants get buried on a Sunday in Lent. Was it a Protestant funeral you were at? Making a disgrace of this family?'

I had no idea. I'd seen the funeral and watched. Catholic, Protestant, I wouldn't know the difference. So I said nothing. I just waited for the beating.

Granny Quinn pulled the door closed behind her and I braced myself.

But this time he didn't beat me straightaway. He just stared at me and told me to go get him something from the shed, then he followed me out. He started to molest me, but I resisted and locked eyes with him just as I grimaced at the smell of his breath. I believe it was a fit of self-loathing took him over and instead he beat me up and down the yard until I passed out.

When I woke up, I had been dragged back into the house and left in the corner of the kitchen. The bruises of his grip were on my arm and leg.

***

Just before I was sent away, not long before I confided in an adult for the first time and was betrayed by them, I got the beating of my life. It was one of those times that no matter how many times I run over the events leading up to it, I cannot for the life of me see where I went wrong.

We were expecting a visit from Marty's aunts. They were two spinsters who lived beyond, in Ballinastore. One was called 'Biddy' I think. I don't remember the other one's name but it might come to me.

They visited once in a while, or we visited them. I was always glad to go because they lived in a house attached to a sweet shop, and you'd go through the shop with its huge jars of glassy humbugs or apple drops to get to the living room. I liked the look of it and I would always hope they would stop and open a jar on our way by, but I've no memory of that ever happening at all. I overheard my mother tell my granny, one time, that they were mean. When they came to visit us, they always kept their hats on and bags on their laps and they never stayed longer than one cup of tea.

This time, I was sweeping the floors and wiping down the surfaces, and then I was kneeling down to clean the hearth. I think I was lost in a daydream when I was suddenly being dragged back by my jumper and then pulled up to stand facing a raging bull.

Marty, in a black rage, reared back and thumped me in the stomach, and then brought his hand straight up to box me on the side of my head over and over until I stumbled sideways and fell on the floor. I shielded myself, turned my back to take the blows as they rained down. The grunts and hisses of the effort it took were the only sounds from him, and I kept as quiet as I could, knowing that crying or screaming would end with his hand strapped across your mouth and nose till you'd nearly pass out.

Balled fists banged down on top of me, on my back, on the top and side of my head. My brain shook. I started feeling sharp stings inside my body, on my back where my kidneys are, so I half turned towards him. I remember thinking, maybe if I smile he will stop, so I tried it.

'I'm sorry,' I said and smiled. He drew back his hand and

slapped me across the head so hard I spun completely around, landing on my hands and feet, taking a kick to the stomach as I did. I staggered to my feet as he caught his breath, hunching from the pain and fear and I put my hands up.

'Stop, stop, I'm so sorry,' I said. It was all I could think to say. I could not figure out what I had done to make him rage, but my face was burning, my back felt broken. With every step forward he took, I took one back. Marty's teeth were bared, like the pictures of the wolves in books I read at school. He kicked my shins and ankles when I found a way to put space between us, making a run for the bedroom and hurling myself onto the bed. I stood up in the corner of the bed, against the wall on the edge of the iron frame. It bit into the soles of my feet through my worn shoes.

But he could still reach me, with a punch to the groin, followed by another one, harder, to the stomach. I called out for my father. I called to him so hard that I fell to my knees on the mattress and got a hard slap that made me bite my tongue. Blood filled my mouth.

Marty pulled me off the bed by the skirt, lashing me across the floor like I was nothing, like a rag. I weighed hardly anything at all. He picked me up by my hair and collar and lashed me against the wall.

'You're a little fucking bastard,' he roared at me and pulled his fist back to bash me with it again, breathing heavily with the exertion of a prize fighter. But there was no fight from me. Marty was beating the life out of a tiny little child. He was no fighter, he was a maniac. He held his fist back to hit me and I noticed his shoulder relax, just a little, and for a sweet moment I thought it was over. But no, he tensed it again, drew it back and sent his fist full force into my jaw knocking my baby teeth out and into my throat.

And after he did that, as I spat teeth onto the mattress, gurgling and gasping, lying there bleeding, he left the room and called out to my mother to 'keep her bastard in check'. I lay in pain and terror that he would return for more. I knew too that he would probably molest me later, he always did, and that made me cry and cry. I wailed.

My mother came in and I saw her briefly shudder as she saw the state of me, but then she acted like I'd simply fallen over.

'Come on now up you get,' she said, and then whispered, 'Don't make things worse, Maureen.'

Worse? I was in so much pain, I didn't think there could be worse. But I agreed with her in principle, only I couldn't stop crying. It was like my lungs were not under my control. The pain in my face and back grew stronger, as the adrenaline of the fight wore off, and with that my wails got louder.

Marty's head came around the door, still out of breath, and said to my mother she would want to shut me up before the aunts arrived. She tried, but I think I was just in a place I couldn't get out of easily. I was miserable and finished and I was calling out for my own father to come and bring me to heaven with him and let me be done with this hell of a life.

'Daddy!' I roared it to the heavens. My mother looked at me like I had lost my mind.

'Shut that up!' she said and slapped me on the legs.

'Shut her up!' Marty said, pointing at me.

My mother stood up and left the room with Marty and I heard her hurried whispers and some fumbling. Then they came back in and stood looking at me.

'Daddy!' I wailed the unfamiliar word again.

Marty snapped his fingers and I looked up. He was holding a ten shilling note up in the air.

I stopped wailing, though my lungs kept the rhythm with loud sobs.

'If you stop crying now, you little bastard, you can have that,' he said. His eyes flicked to the front door. The aunts were never late, you see.

I knew my mother had given it to him. I'd heard the clasp of her purse outside the door. I didn't want to give in. I didn't want to be shut up with money. I wanted the aunts to arrive and ask why I was crying, and then they would see the blood on my mouth and hit Marty with their bags, and I thought of how his face would look when they did. But then I thought of Granny and how her face would look if I gave her ten bob, and all the sweets we could buy for us, so I ran forward, snapped the note off him like a stray dog taking bread from a human hand, and retreated back to the corner of the bed.

My mother came in then with a flannel and washed my face. She didn't say anything. The aunts' knock came. I was quiet and I stayed there, with my bruised face and swollen jaw, toothless and bleeding, hidden away in the bedroom clutching my ten bob in my fist, pressed against my heart like I would never let go of it.

5

SHAY

I didn't know I was living a life of fear. I didn't understand the things I do now, that my feelings and actions at that time were those of a traumatised child, one living in a state of constant and unrelenting terror. It was the pulse of my heart and the basis of every choice I made.

Every irritant in Marty's life was solved with attacks on us. I don't remember if he hit the others. I don't remember ever seeing him lay a hand on one of his own. I never once saw that that I can remember. I'll be honest here about it and anyway, if he did, that's their story to tell. I'll just tell my own story how I remember it. That's all I can do.

He called us bastards, dissolving the marriage of my parents in his head, refusing to acknowledge that we three were the children of her first husband, the real one. The one she wanted.

If the fire was low, or the milk was gone off, he would blame us Sullivans. He decided which one of us was at fault and punished that one, usually the nearest one to him. Or if he discovered the error when we were not home, he would sit and bull, then go for the first one of us through the door. Marty never took himself down to the shop to get household items. He never found an empty milk can so concerning that he made his own way to buy more. No, he sat and stewed on the failure of his wife, or her first husband's children, to have everything sorted at all times. And when she didn't, or we didn't, he battered *us*.

So we learned that coming home was often a game of Russian roulette – you didn't know if Marty was in a mood or not. We tried to stay ahead of him, never relaxing, always making sure that everything was done and dusted. The fire was always lit and left burning, with fuel piled nearby. The milk was always checked in advance and we tried never to let it run out. Thankfully we lived in a time when you could get a chit in the local shop and pay the bill at the end of the week. The settling of that bill was another reason to be punished. We would all be accused of running it up too high, and at best would be lectured, but a beating would usually come out of it.

I was nervous all day and unsettled all night, except when I was in Granny's. That was the only real rest I ever got.

The beating the day of the aunts' visit led to another. But it wasn't mine. When the aunts went, myself and my two brothers were washing up the cups they'd used in the kitchen. I still had my ten shillings in my hand and was doing everything with a closed fist. The lights were dim and Marty's brother Shay, who had been at the visit, stood up to go. Perhaps prompted by the fact that I would not come to him when he called me to take his cup, perhaps noting my mother's frown and shake of her head to tell me to stay where I was, he said, 'Why aren't you coming to say hello to me when I call you, Maureen?'

I stood there for a minute.

'Maureen, come here to me,' he said again, firmly. I looked at my mother and she nodded so I moved into the light, to where Shay was sitting beside Marty. Shay's face went dark when he saw mine. He sucked air through his teeth and started to shake his head. I ran back and hid behind my brother, Paddy. Shay turned and went through the adjoining door into his own cottage, pulling it closed behind him.

Later, when we children were all in bed and I was barely asleep, lying with my face against the cold wall for pain relief, I heard a raised voice that brought me to my senses. I lifted my head to listen. It was Shay. I heard a bang, a scuffle of feet and grunts and groans. I sat up and pushed my arms through the old coat that acted as my blanket.

I slipped out of bed, taking care to place my feet and hands as I climbed over the other children to the end of the bed and onto the floor, crossed the floor and leaned against the doorframe, pressing my eye against the crack to see into the room. Shay had Marty over the table, knocking his head into the plate of dinner that Marty had been eating. My mother was nowhere to be seen. I imagined her shadow in the kitchen.

Shay hissed, 'You will leave those kids alone, you bullying bastard. Give it up!'

He throttled Marty against the table, his full weight pinning Marty down, one leg straight behind him, the other bent against the table. Marty managed to turn himself, and his chair, balancing on two legs, slid forward, knocking them both off balance and giving Marty enough leverage to get to his feet. Then Shay punched Marty in the face. Spit flew out of his mouth and his eyes closed with a wince. I was glad. Shay stood back but Marty didn't advance, he stayed where he was.

'They're children, you fucking bastard,' Shay said, rushing forward again and throwing him against the door of the bedroom I was in. I scuttled back to the bed, climbed back in, terrified that they would spill through the door on top of us. But the fight carried on outside the door and they rolled around and boxed each other, Marty roaring that Shay should mind his own business and Shay roaring that Marty was to leave us alone and leave my mother alone.

I pressed my hands together and prayed to the crucifix above my head, asking God to intervene.

'Please God, please God, please,' I whispered with as much Catholic devotion as could ever have been stirred in that little body of mine. I prayed and prayed, rolling the learned words over in my mouth, *ourfatherwhoartinheavenhallowedbethyname.* I named saints and fruits of wombs, and called on every angel I could remember, squeezing my eyes shut to make it count.

But I wasn't praying they would stop. I was praying Shay would go on and on until there was nothing left of Marty Murphy.

I was praying that Shay would kill him.

***

Not long after that we were given an offer of a three-bedroom council house just down the way a bit in Roncalli Place. We no longer fit, as a family, in the two-room cottage in Green Lane, so it made sense and we moved in.

Our house in Roncalli Place was block built and two storeys, with a covered door on the side and its own garden enclosed in a fence made of iron posts with long iron poles running length-ways, and a gate. There was a bathroom, with a bath and toilet that had mains water directly into them. I could not believe my eyes – flushing the toilet was miraculous to me. And we had three bedrooms now, so the boys were in their own room. The walk to school was shorter as Roncalli Place is just across the road from Scoil Mhuire gan Smal, as my school is called now, still there on the crossroads of Accommodation Road and Green Lane.

But apart from the bathroom and a bit more room in the beds, nothing changed for me at all, except that having an upstairs part to the house meant that isolating me was a little easier for Marty.

6

MAUREEN THE LIAR

Marty called me a liar the first night he molested me. I walked by him after, and in a loud voice he said, 'Well if it isn't Maureen the liar.' It stopped me in my tracks, and I waited for the accusation to continue, but that was all he had to say. He just looked me dead in the eyes with a horrible smirk on his face.

Then he said it again, 'Maureen the liar.'

I don't think he referred to me again without tagging that on. I used to wonder what he meant, what lies had I told. I mean, I knew I did lie; I told my granny I fell when she asked me why I was rubbing my hip. I didn't want to tell her the truth, that Marty had kicked me and left a bruise. I told my teacher I had forgotten to do my homework once or twice, when I had done it but Marty had pulled the pages apart in a temper at the scraping noise of my pencil. I told my mother I had a pain in my stomach to try to get her to stay home and not go to work because I knew what was ahead of me if she did.

Those were the lies I told.

But I knew Marty didn't know about those, and I knew intuitively something else was going on with that new nickname. I knew he was saying it for a reason, for something that was confusing. I know now he was gaslighting me. He said it so often that everyone picked up on it. One day my mother even said, 'Maureen, is this another one of your lies?' Apart from pretending to be ill I had never lied to my mother in my life.

Mud sticks, they say.

Paedophiles do whatever they can to be able to keep abusing children. Marty knew there was a chance I would either slip up and tell someone something weird about him, or that I would reach my limit and tell my whole story. Maybe he considered the idea that my granny would accuse him to my mother. He had his defence well set up: sure, isn't Maureen a terrible liar. Even now that name follows me, even these days people I grew up with will still insist I tell lies. Well, that's for them to say, and to be honest it's none of my business if they want to say that, let them. My story belongs to me and it is not a lie. I've had my story torn apart by the redress board and a judge found every bit of it to be truthful.

Marty's manipulation added a huge pressure to my life that caused me great pain and the horrible stress of injustice. The smaller kids picked up on that nickname quick and it spread into school and I became 'Maureen the liar' there too. There was nothing I could do about it. My reputation as a child was what he painted me and it gave other children the upper hand. They did what they liked to me and got away with it because Maureen's the liar. So I never fought against it. I was so worn out at that point I didn't see the point anyway. I just carried on and hoped something terrible would happen to him.

I wasn't the only one. My brothers were painted in similar ways and struggled because of it too. Marty told the Christian Brothers on day one that Michael was a handful and prone to violence, and they went extra hard on him because of that. They beat him sometimes within an inch of his life, but Michael would never submit. He was my father's son, strong and good, and he always got back up when he was knocked down. Eventually when they couldn't break him they sent him away to Artane Industrial School, like they would send me away to the laundry.

The memories of my childhood and teens come to me in blocks when I look for them. They start on one part and end on the other, with mostly blur in between. I think we are all like that. But then there are the ones that creep in when I'm not thinking of anything. Sometimes I flinch from a flying hand that isn't there because I am on my own, in my own home. Sometimes I feel the stirrings of the same fear I felt as a child when I noticed a look or heard a footstep, even though I am safe, locked twice into my own house. Marty's violence and depravity has impacted my entire life and always will – no matter how much I work through it, no matter how much I reassure my inner child that he is burning in hell. I was tormented by that man as a child and I am still tormented. I never had a say in any of it.

When he comes into my mind, and he often does, I shake. I'm shaking now telling this story – it's a reaction. For years though, I didn't speak about what Marty did to me, what he took away from me – the years I had bottled it all up, sworn to take it to the grave with me, the whole thing. For years it was like I was living a pretend life, where this didn't happen to me. I'm glad I'm not living that way now, even though at times this is harder. That life would have ended me for sure. It almost did a few times, if I am honest with you.

Now, when I think of him, it's as if his shadow comes into the room, the same one I'd see on the bed when the bedroom door opened, the one I'd see move in the sunlight on the floor taking his braces off as I crouched in the corner. That shadow was how I knew my day was up, that shadow was how I knew I was in for something.

The dread of the noise of those braces, the way the elastic sounded against the material of his shirt sleeves, it was like the hiss of a demon. I hear that hiss in my nightmares. I get flash-backs of the sound of the door of our house when I was coming home from school, knowing my mother was at work. I'd push the door open and the light would reveal whether Marty was home or not. The pure relief when he was not, the spike of fear when he was. I can hear him, the strange shuffle as he hobbled around the clay floors of Green Lane. I can see him, his thin body in wide-leg trousers that gave him bulk, fists balled up in the sleeves of his jacket, furious. The smell of smoke and pigs from his clothing.

He would say, 'Maureen, throw a dash of coffee under my chin,' and I would imagine throwing the scalding cup into his face. If I could go back now I would do it. I wanted to spit in that coffee, but I never had the nerve. The pot never boiled fast enough for Marty. The coffee he drank turned his breath sour. His tongue tasted of it.

More than once my anxiety would manifest in twisting pains in my stomach that were so bad my mother would take me to the doctor. I did get constant urine infections and other infections below. My insides were bruised and torn up. I was wetting the bed because going to the toilet often hurt so much.

But there is that *one* lie I told a lot. Even when I felt fine I told my mother I had stomach pain anyway, just so she would take me out of the house and bring me to the doctor.

7

THE HOSPITAL

Doctor Callaghan's surgery was bright and safe, and so was he. I loved him. I loved how he put his hands under my arms and lifted me onto his long leather examining bed that was against the wall of his surgery. He had the walls painted yellow and there were posters of the insides of the human body. I was fascinated by those. There were medical books on shelves and a big desk with things in zip-up leather cases that he would use to look in my ears and mouth.

I loved the feel of Doctor Callaghan's hands as he pressed my tummy. I loved that so much I would often forget to pretend to feel pain. He always warmed his hands up by blowing into them with a loud 'Haw' sound, and then pressed around with one hand on the other to find the source of my agony. He never moved my knickers without asking my mother and me. I knew the difference between good men and bad, even back then.

On one occasion where I lied so convincingly about being in pain, Doctor Callaghan sent me by ambulance to Our Lady's

Hospital in Crumlin in Dublin. It was a brand-new hospital back then and I may as well have been going on a holiday. I tell you, I was absolutely charmed with myself. My mother bought me a new nightdress, so as not to be judged by the pristine sisters who ran the hospital with keen eyes and noses for dirt.

The cost of that nightdress was used against me many times by Marty – how much I owed for it, what it cost, how everyone had to go without to buy nighties for Maureen the liar. He was so angry when I got back from Dublin, he was bent up with frustration from the lack of access to me, I think.

He made up for that.

But I did stay in the hospital for a long time, I'm sure at least six weeks, and even though all my tests were clear they took my appendix out anyway. It was something to do to end the riddle of my pain.

Being in hospital was traumatic for most of my ward mates. But not for me. I sat in my bed knowing that Marty Murphy could not come in there. He was not allowed. When I first arrived I asked the nurse who put me into bed on the first night could people's stepfathers come in, and she told me not at all, and she looked at me for a long time and then brought me toast and tea with sugar in it.

Most of the other children there missed their mothers and would cry into the night with homesickness. I swear I thought they were ridiculous. That hospital, for me, was a blessed respite, a huge relief. We got three good meals a day, plus a snack. We had poached fish and cabbage, chicken and lamb with potatoes. At lunch we got good soup and soft bread. Breakfast was bowls of hot porridge, and you could put your own sugar on. It was not as nice as granny's goody, but it was good enough.

We got fruit – grapes and apples and even oranges. And we got jelly. I couldn't believe anyone would be crying about this place.

Light came in the window, and fresh air, and there was warmth from the huge radiators beneath them and soft cosy silver beds to ourselves. There was a mechanism the nurses would pull up so you could sit, and they'd wheel us out for fresh air along this large veranda at the front. We had blankets and crisp sheets laid over us fresh every day, and we were tucked in at night after we peed in the pot that the nurse would take away for testing. Kind hands washed us in the bath, in hot clean water with soap, and we were checked for health and stood onto scales and kept warm.

The only time I cried there was when I thought about going home.

The nurses there wore white uniforms, dresses to the knee with pristine collars and white hats, and most of them had their hair short and set. They were like angels in my eyes. Dotted in with them were one or two nuns. If my memory serves me they were dressed in black versions of the same, with short, white veils. And I think the matron was in a full habit, which included a winged wimple that made her look like a statue when she was caught in the light.

The little girl in the bed next to me, with her long brown plaits and a patch on one eye, let me play with her doll. It was one of those fat little dolls with short blonde hair and a little pink dress. I'd seen her grandmother bring it in a bag, though nobody was allowed visitors in the ward. I had seen her out the window. Her grandmother wore a hat, a wool coat and had a shiny brooch on her lapel. I had no visitors and that was fine with me, although I missed my granny and wished I could tell her I was getting to have jelly and blancmange. I loved the jelly.

In the hospital all of us children were the same. There was no way for anyone to tell that I was the poor child or that my ward mate was well off. My nightie was washed every evening the same as the other children's, and I was washed too, every day, like everyone else. We were equals and that meant I felt really free to be myself, to play and talk to other children in a way I never felt at home.

When the Matron told me I was going home it felt like I had been put on death row. Back to that house, back to that filthy man. I wanted to die. I told the nurses the pain was back, but they knew it wasn't.

'Do you love jelly that much, Maureen, that you don't want to go home?' one of them asked me.

The little girl beside me went first, just by a few days, and she put the fat doll on my bed before she left. I was delighted.

That doll was taken off me as soon as my foot crossed the door at home.

***

Did the nurses discuss me and my phantom pains and wonder what was going on at home that a small child like me would prefer the hospital to my own place? They saw the evidence, surely, of my abuse. When I got there, I must have been covered in bruises. I always was. I was examined there by two doctors, looking for the source of pain, and they would have seen bruising at the tops of my legs and my groin. They surely saw the fear in my face when they told me I was going home.

They had to have suspected *something*.

So I'll ask now, what were the criteria for raising a red flag for abuse in Ireland in 1960? Because I suspect that *'poor female child'* was not on the list.

8

THE CAMPAIGN

In those days, Carlow was a main producer of sugar beet and every year the harvests would bring the entire county to life, with all hands on deck to get the beets in. This was known as 'the campaign'.

From the harvest in September until December, the lumpy white root vegetable that looks something like a huge fat parsnip was king. Every generation of families was involved, from the children crawling on sack-covered knees in the dirt to pull the weeds, to the grown-ups coming behind them with a knife to pull the vegetable by hand, cut the greens away and load the root into piles in the backs of the square wooden trains that brought them stacked high to the factory for processing by whoever could get a spot in there that year. It was an exercise that went on all day and all night, seven days a week.

I have faded memories of the campaign from my young days, and really most of what I know about it is through my brother Paddy, because my story takes me out of Carlow aged twelve and I never really got back to it until that was all over and the factories were closed down.

Beet was known as a 'cash crop', in that farmers were paid an advance, and that trickled down into the pockets of the people. For the few months of the campaign, Carlow was fat, and everyone in it was tired but in great form.

Once the beet was in, it was washed and juiced and then a process would take place that boiled off the sugar. The smell in the air during the campaign from the clouds of sugar smoke that pumped out the chimneys was like candyfloss at a fun fair.

Some lads worked at the factories full time, all year round, and piles of apprentices and permanent full-timers worked there. But then, besides that, there would be those 'permanent campaign workers', men like Marty, who returned every year just for that period and were guaranteed work for six to eight weeks of the campaign in the processing plant. It was good money and it had the effect of an excuse – for the want of a better word – for Marty not to have a job. For the rest of the year he played about with scrap and sold pigs, but mostly he just sat around. The money paid out for those six weeks made him feel like he was justified in his unemployment, it was so good for that short time.

The county and everyone in it thrived in those months. Everyone had money in their pockets, including us. And after chits were paid up and things were got that were needed, there'd often be some left and there would be meat in the dinner every night for that time at least. Everyone in the county did a little better. And for those weeks that Marty was gone, the three Sullivan kids did a little better too. First, he was gone from the house all the time, which of course meant less abuse and full access to our granny, and second, food was available. It also meant we had the campaign workers' Christmas party to look forward to.

The party was held every year in the Ritz picture house and ballroom. It was a grand building on Tullow Street in the town, built on the site of an old hotel and retaining the ballroom, which is where the party was. There would be food and drinks that were only dreams in the average Carlow child's life for the rest of the year: lemonade or fizzy orange, piles of fairy cakes made by farmers' wives and their baking circles. There were bowls of fruit and bowls of sweets and plates of white iced biscuits that cracked when you bit into them. Then, at the end, you got a small present from Santa. That would be our only present from Santa.

I remember seeing my mother writing my name on the ticket form. She wrote 'Maureen Murphy' and so I corrected her, 'Mammy, that's not right, I'm Maureen Sullivan,' I said.

'Ah Maureen, that'll cause confusion,' she said. 'They'll be asking are we one Sullivan or another. We won't cause a fuss this way, alright?' And she put the top back on the pen.

I didn't want to be a Murphy. Seeing my name written that way made me sad and anxious. I wanted only to be John L. Sullivan's daughter, the prize-fighting army deserter from Bennekerry, my granny's son. I wanted nothing of Marty Murphy, that monster, not even his name for one night. It made me sick.

What I loved the most about the campaign was – because Marty was gone – we had unfettered access to Granny Sullivan. Most days Granny Quinn would come up to the house so my mother could go to her job, and if I was there, I would help her with the babies. But my Granny Sullivan had wily ways and often she would knock in and give an excuse to take me and my brothers. She would bring us with her to work in the fields, thinning the beets out for the men to pull.

I don't remember it exactly – I was young and the memory has faded – but I do remember Granny's voice calling down to me as I kneeled in the muck with something to protect my knees. 'Good girl,' she said, 'well done,' and 'You're a great farmer so you are.' I wanted so badly to hear Granny tell me those things I got carried away, went too fast and fell face first into the muck, and Granny had to pull me out by the scruff of my neck. She was laughing and kissing my cheeks as she wiped the soil off.

'Well,' she said, 'were you trying to plant yourself? Sure aren't you the sweetest bit of sugar I have?'

I loved time spent with my granny. Even hard work was the best time when she was close.

***

When the beet factories closed down, we lost the heart of Carlow. The sweetness went out of the air.

9

COWBOYS
AND INDIANS

The house in Green Lane, in my memory, had a yard that ran up one side and around the back of the house. There were pig pens up the very back. Keeping pigs was a good way to bring in some extra money once or twice a year. People bought two bonhams for a few pence at the start of the year and fed them small potatoes and grain for the year, and then sold them at the pig fair for a profit. Most people did that.

We always did too, in Green Lane, and I would always get attached to the little bonhams that would be put in the sty to fatten up and be sold. By the third round of them, I stopped playing with them as soon as the summer ended as I couldn't take letting them go. They were sweet animals. Nothing sleeps as sound as a pig. Their big pink bodies relax into the mud, and for me, as a little worn-out child, those pigs were a comfort. They didn't mind me. Their soft noses would search for my hand when I got in with them, headbutting me gently to see if I had a scrap. I never did. But sometimes I would spot a small potato in the corner of their trough that they had missed and catch it out for them. They loved me for that, I suppose. When they slept, they snored, and sometimes on warm days I would climb in and nap there with them, my head in the crease of their legs, feeling the rise and fall against my cheek of their huge lungs. The sounds they'd make, the little snuffles and snorts as they dreamt – animals are a great comfort.

**

Marty kept scrap and old cars in the yard. His hands were permanently black from oil, but in my memory there was nothing more than a pile of bits and pieces that he tinkered with when he felt like it. I never remember him selling anything, although I'm sure he did. He also didn't drive a car after I was about five or six, not that I remember anyway, but I know my mother said he drove one when they first courted. Saying that, he never had one in my memory, not after I was about six.

The yard was a playground on the days of the campaign, days when Marty wasn't home and we knew he wouldn't be. His schedule was set. Being off the hook, coming in from school knowing you wouldn't be caught by his hand as you did, gave us a sort of high. I was off the hook in other ways too – the campaign kept Marty out late and I slept by the wall so he wouldn't usually get a chance to molest me.

Paddy and me, we loved to play in the old cars that were in the yard, some of them on blocks, some with wheels, giving make-believe a good go.

This one day we were halfway across the prairies of the Wild West, with Indians and cowboys in hot pursuit. We hadn't quite decided if we had robbed a bank, but that was likely, and so, like a miniature Bonnie and Clyde we shot back at our pursuers with our fingers, killing loads of them and shouting, 'I got one, I got one,' as we flew through the desert dust to freedom. Buffalo Bill, John Wayne, every character we could think of was after us, and I cried out, 'Get him, Paddy,' and put my foot down, speeding the car into the sun.

All of a sudden, my enthusiastic driving efforts knocked the handbrake off and the car we were in began to roll forward, down the slope of the yard and towards the road. And as with all good horror films – which our western was swiftly turning into – Marty Murphy, the real-life villain, stepped into view, a dark shadow that took shape as he turned the corner into the lane to our house.

We both jolted back into reality, filled with absolute terror as we saw the cut of him. We were headed straight for him in a slow roll.

He didn't see us, not straight away. He didn't notice the approaching pioneer wagon with its outlaw occupants, as his back was to us, looking down the road at something, but then I shrieked and he looked over his shoulder and for the first and only time in my life I saw fear cross Marty Murphy's face.

It didn't last long.

I suppose at first, until his brain registered our slow speed, he saw something like comeuppance. The kids he beat crooked taking revenge in a car. He might have thought we were driving to kill him, to run him down, to do him in. God knows, but he did look afraid for a moment.

But, of course, he realised the car was rolling at the pace of a snail, and so he simply stood out of the way and we rolled on by and down the yard until the flat tyres lost the momentum our bouncing bodies had given it further up and the car came to a miserable and sighing halt.

Jesus, me and Paddy hopped out of that car and tore up the road. We were so certain that Marty would come after us, we didn't even look back and we ran and ran and ran until our lungs bate us and we rolled into a ditch. We were fully sure Marty was a step behind us as we collapsed and we tensed up for the blows that were going to come. Surely he would beat us dead now.

But he didn't.

Our lungs were burning and we spoke to each other in wheezy belts between sucking in air, our hands on our knees, bent over in the ditch. We stayed there for ages, lying up the verge on our bellies, propped up on elbows watching through the gaps in the hedge as pickers picked the potatoes from the ground after the spinner went through the soil. The sun caught the rows and striped the field in brown and black and you could see workers' shadows in the halo of its light. When they were all gone, in the evening, we crawled through those gaps like commandoes and filled Paddy's pockets and my sleeves with potatoes they had stacked along the rows. We stashed them then, further up, to take to Granny's.

We snuck back in later, as soon as we reckoned Marty was in his chair by the fire with his coffee cup in his hand. We dashed from the back door to the beds, got under the coats and lay still.

He never said anything about it.

10

THE CHOCOLATE BAR

In Mr and Mrs Sharkey's shop in Bennekerry, in the window, there was – among other things – a giant-sized bar of Cadbury's Dairy Milk chocolate. It was the size of the big atlas we had in our school. My brothers and I waited for Granny outside that shop, with our noses stuck into the glass of that window, wishing it was ours. Our foreheads would be pink from pressing them against the glass, fruitlessly trying to get closer to the dream. There was a navy wrapper with 'Cadbury's' in joined-up writing, and the bar itself was wrapped in gold foil.

'I'd have it ate in one minute,' I'd say, and my brothers would argue that wasn't possible, and all sorts of calculations would go on about how long it might take to get the whole thing into your belly.

'You'd have it ate in ten minutes,' they decided.

We always looked at it, and always talked about what we would do with it, how fast we could eat it or how long we could make it last, adding up how many squares we thought there was against how many days you could stretch it out. We divided it up, shared it out in our minds, even fought over it. We talked about how sick we might be if we ate it all at once, but there was three of us, we would be grand.

'That bar is torture,' Paddy always said.

***

One morning, at a weekend when we were at Granny's, she sent us down to Sharkey's to get the messages. Usually she went with us on the way home from school on the Friday, but this time, for whatever reason, she sent us back up to the shop once we got home. We loved an errand from Granny. She trusted us with her money and she always forgave mistakes if we made them, or if we forgot something.

She treated us like children.

This one morning, Michael went in to get whatever it was on the list that Granny asked for, and myself and Paddy stayed outside. Suddenly Michael, after finding the shop empty and no sign of Mr or Mrs Sharkey at all, flew by us running, head down, full pelt, with that huge bar of Cadbury's Dairy Milk under his arm. He was away, yelling as he ran by to us, 'Run!' and God bless us and save us, we ran like the wind after him, up the hill as fast as we could. My poor hips started to seize, so I lagged a little, but I ignored the pain and kept going. I didn't think I had it in me, but I didn't want to fall behind the lads and leave them to eat that whole bar in ten minutes, like they swore they would, without me. I had to catch up with that prize, so I buckled down and kept going.

I saw my brothers spin into a field, and when I caught up,

they were giggling, rolling in the grass, whooping and thumping each other on the back and arms. Michael held the bar up above his head like it was a trophy. None of us could speak, none of us could breathe. This was it. We gathered in under the overgrown hedgerow and hunkered down. I squeezed in between the two of them. I couldn't believe we had it. That bar of chocolate was ours – our dream had come true. There was a bit of arguing about who should open it. It became a rights issue between Michael and Paddy, but I couldn't have cared less who did, I just wanted a piece of it. My mouth was watering. None of us thought about the fact that we were now criminals. We had stolen from a shop we were in and out of all the time. None of us thought about the Sharkey's or if we could be caught, we just wanted the chocolate.

'I'll open it,' I said to prompt them to just decide, and it worked. Michael said no, it was his bar and if we wanted any we should shut up. So we did. Michael pulled the foil-covered bar from the navy paper wrapper and then scraped the foil away with his nail, and tore it open, pulling the foil away to reveal the contents beneath.

We had been tricked.

It took us a moment or two to realise what it was that we were looking at, but we knew instantly it wasn't chocolate. It was a grey flecked slab of something else.

It was a prop. It was made of cardboard.

Michael ripped the cardboard in two, one last desperate prayer that the actual chocolate was inside but no, it was empty. Not so much as a crumb. We had been scammed.

By the time we recovered from the shock and slunk back to Granny's – gone far too long and arriving without the messages – she had heard.

She asked us straight out, 'Did you take that bar from Sharkey's?'

My brothers attempted to lie. They shook their heads, but I burst out, 'Granny, it was feckin' cardboard!'

I yelled it out, so disappointed and incensed that we had – I felt – been conned. I spilled my guts. I told her the whole story in one long wail.

Granny's eyes went round, 'Well,' she said and then pressed her mouth closed really tight and turned away, covering her mouth with both of her hands. I thought she must be let down, disgusted with us. I reached out and tugged her dress at the waist. Her shoulders were shaking and she was making little whimper sounds, pressing her hand across her mouth and refusing to turn to me even though I pulled at her. I thought she was crying and so I started crying.

She finally spoke, wiping tears from her eyes and she said, 'Well, that's a lesson for ye, three thieves I have in my house. Well, that'll teach you!' And I thought for a moment from her eyes that she was going to smile, but she covered her face up again with her hands and turned away again.

I felt so bad for making Granny cry. I threw my brothers dagger eyes as I stood there pulling on Granny's dress trying to see her face, trying to see the damage I had done. That bar had really ruined my day.

Granny washed her face and our faces and put her coat on and walked us all down to Sharkey's shop to get the things we had not, and when we got there Mr and Mrs Sharkey were in a flap. Mrs Sharkey was questioning people when they came in, telling them about the robbery, asking if they saw anything.

Nobody had.

Mrs Sharkey said, 'The chocolate people don't give those props out to just anyone.'

She questioned Granny. She told her, 'If we find out who took that bar, they will be sorry. Mr Sharkey will beat them AND call the Guards. They'd go to court for that, maybe even jail.'

I shook in my boots, twisting Granny's coat in my fist. I hadn't considered jail.

Granny said to Mrs Sharkey that she thought perhaps someone had taken it out of spite. She asked Mrs Sharkey if she thought that another shopkeeper might have crept in, in a planned way, and stolen it. Maybe they were jealous, you know, because those bars weren't given to everyone.

Mrs Sharkey's face puckered and her eyes went to slivers. She seemed to roll the idea over in her mouth.

'Do you think, Katie?' she said.

Granny said she did.

Mrs Sharkey came round to that. She was pleased to think of that. 'You might be right, Katie,' she said and pursed her mouth and made a little clucking sound. 'You might actually be right.'

***

That evening, after our dinner, Granny had a chocolate sweet for each of us.

11

DAYS OUT

I don't remember much about school. Flashes of playing and listening, mostly just one or two scenes in my head that don't last long.

We wore blue at our little school, little gymslips with white shirts and blue cardigans. There is a photo of me somewhere, taken by a teacher. I'm sitting on a chair in front of the church. I'm thin.

I mostly tried to stay to myself in school. I knew there was something different about me. I knew that from the first day I started there. I'd seen our teacher, Sister Cecilia, lift her nose to the air and then wander down around the classroom, pretending to sweep the floors so she could source the smell of pee. I knew from the way girls unfolded wrapped sandwiches, peeling back tinfoil off the sticky soft white bread, and opened flasks full of hot tea at lunchtime that I was different. I didn't have school lunch. I had nothing to eat.

'Did you forget your lunch?' one girl asked me one time as

she held a jam sandwich to my nose. I reached out for it and she snatched it back away.

On Fridays, when Granny collected us from school, or from home if we had to bring the younger ones back, sometimes she would take us up beyond to the woods at Duckett's Grove. Duckett's Grove has always been, in my lifetime, an abandoned castle at the end of an impossibly long drive, but it was lived in once. The gates at the start of the drive are huge, Gothic and grey, and as a child I was frightened by them, reminded of witches in stories, but the castle itself felt magical.

By the time we arrived we would be starving, bellies aching for something to eat. Granny would lead us past the castle itself, pointing at the crows and warning us never to cross them, then down the little worn paths through the woods to the old green tunnel. It is still behind the castle there. She'd sit us down on the ground and take wrapped paper packets from the huge pocket of her apron, one by one. I loved the look of her hands, her crooked fingers, as she fiddled with the paper twists to open them. Inside there would be cut apple and hunks of white bread spread with jam and sandwiched together. That food would be wolfed down.

'Will ye watch now ye don't choke,' Granny would say, 'I'll take that bread off you now, if you don't mind yourself when you're eating.' It was a threat that worked. We chewed really slowly when Granny said that.

I don't know if you have ever had the privilege to set eyes on Duckett's Grove, but even as an adult it strikes awe into me every time I see it. I go there often with my little dog and walk around again, thinking of how wonderful it was to grow up so close to such an extraordinary place. It is a castle built by one of Ireland's rich Protestant families, who had more money than they knew how to spend. The history of it is written on plaques down there. Now, thankfully, it belongs to Carlow and is maintained by the people as a public space.

As a child it was paradise. We would play among the trees and run around the castle – me and Paddy would be Robin Hood and Little John fighting the sheriff. Dodging arrows and horses all the way, we would race back to the safety of the forest beyond, where Granny would be waiting, still sitting on the little shelf inside the tunnel resting her shoulder against the old stone.

Granny always let us go up there. She never interrupted play unless there was a shoelace untied or a coat unbuttoned. Then her hand would fly up and she would bring us swiftly back to reality with a sharp 'Ah ah', until we gave her our attention and she could tie the lace or button the coat again and let us go.

And when my brothers would leave me behind and race away to climb trees or do things I couldn't because of my injuries, my granny would sit down there in the tunnel with me and play.

'You be Mrs O'Brien now,' she would say to me, starting to sweep up an imaginary house. Granny worked for a Mrs O'Brien, a farmer's wife, on a casual basis, cleaning and making dinners and looking after their cows when they needed her. They'd send down word that she was needed with one of their workers, who came on a bike.

I took on that role with gusto. 'Now, Katie,' I'd say with the thrill of a child dropping formalities, 'can you sweep behind there now?'

'Yes Ma'am,' my granny said, and curtsied. I knew she never

curtsied to Mrs O'Brien, and I knew she never called her ma'am either. Granny made me laugh.

'Katie,' I'd say, pointing at an imaginary window, 'now that needs to be cleaned so I can see out at all my cows you know.' I stretched my voice up high to make it posh.

'Yes Ma'am.'

'And you'd want to be getting on with our dinner,' I'd say.

'Yes Ma'am,' Granny would say, 'what would you like?'

'Ham and ... peas,' I'd say knowing what would come next if I did.

'Oooo, yes Ma'am, no Ma'am, and Ma'am if you please,' she would wink, 'and it's up the duck's arse you can stick your green peas!'

Without fail I would fall onto the ground hearing that, laughing so hard I would start to cough.

Sometimes Granny would stop us at the castle and we would sit on the old doorway together as my brothers ran races across the vast lawn.

'Now, Maureen,' she would say, 'you be the queen.'

'What will you be, Granny?'

'I'll be the queen's granny,' she would say.

In that place, and everywhere we went with Granny, we were free. Free of beatings, free of abuse, free of the responsibilities loaded on older siblings in those days. We were free to run around, to find adventures and interest.

***

On hotter days Granny would take us down to the river in Bennekerry, at a spot where the sides of the Burren river had worn away the land, just by the bridge, where it was safe for swimming. My brothers loved it. They'd stay in the water for ages. I was a little more cautious, but I still loved to go there.

I preferred when it was quiet though, when it wasn't a really sunny day when half of Bennekerry would be out at the river. I hated when it was packed because I was embarrassed at the old, stained towel Granny brought with her, even though it was clean. The yellow and brown stains on a grey rag. Was it ever white? Granny used to dry the three of us with that towel down at the river, and I used to be embarrassed of that. Once I saw some girls from my class down there and they made a face when they saw me.

It's funny how even as children we can see our differences. I knew I had stains on my socks and a dirty collar. I knew Granny's towel was old and stained. And it mattered to me.

Where did I learn that? My brothers never seemed to care, or my mother. Granny sure didn't. But I did. And I knew Granny was right when she told me not to mind them. She was always right. But snobbery affected me. I felt terrible back then, six or probably seven, standing in my stained pants on the edge of a brown river in the sunshine, wishing I could disappear.

When we were at the river and nobody was around I would strip to my knickers along with my brothers and go into the coppery soft water. It was freezing around my knees, but eventually my legs would go numb and I'd walk around, feeling the smooth stones and sand under my feet. I'd watch out for the tiny darting fish. I'd bend and trace the water with my fingertips, wondering how it was so clear in the palm of my hand but so brown when all together as a river. On the far side I'd watch a kingfisher, pointed out by Granny who had spied it. She told me it was a fairy dressed as a bird, and I believed it – a tiny, bright-blue thing that was gone as soon as it came.

Sometimes I would worry about the big brown fish that I had seen pulled out of that river by the fisherman on the bridge and I'd curl my toes under my feet in fear of their mouths. My brothers looked for gold, sieving the sand between their fingers. I pretended too. The ends of my hair were wet from bending to look into the water.

I stopped going into water at all after that summer. I fell from the bank of the Burne river, up our way, while scuttling down it after my older brother Michael. I slipped onto my back in the soft ground and found no purchase in the wet grass. It was another river altogether from the one Granny preferred. We shouldn't have been there. She'd always warned us because the water was deeper there and ran faster. When I fell, I clutched at the grass in vain, sliding all the way down until I was fully under the water. When I think of it, I can see myself surrounded by black waters, a little white sprite reaching up in a shaft of light but going further down into the blackness. In my memory I became still, looking up at the surface of the water, the bubbles from my thrashing legs disappearing one by one. I heard my brother calling me, muffled through the surface.

One gasp – oh the pain of that – and one thought, *I don't want to be dead.*

But I was pulled out or climbed out, for the next I knew I was on the bank, heaving and screaming. The pain in your lungs when they are trying to rid themselves of water is intense. It's so intense you can't get away from it, and can't move or think or see.

Michael was banging me on the back. I heard him cursing. I held my hand up, but he banged away. I coughed and gasped. On the bridge a fisherman pulled a flapping trout from the water.

12

THE HALF CROWN

Granny was poor as a church mouse. She got a tiny pension on a Friday, but after she paid for the basics, she had nothing left. But she did her best to do without during the week so she could have good food for us at the weekend. I can imagine her frustrations, seeing her grandchildren neglected and starved but being unable to do anything about it. She wouldn't risk it, so she attempted to balance it out with fat and meat at the weekend.

She showed her love for us in all ways. She would creep out of bed early, leaving us sleeping on cold mornings, in those freezing hours when the condensation from our breath on the windows was ice. Wearing her coat and hunkered down on the mud floor she would get the fire started and going before we woke up. There was a draft that came under the door that would cut your legs in two as you raced out of the bedroom, so the fire was a relief.

That fire went all day in the winter, and only faded in the

early hours of the night. Granny would cover the dying embers in wet paper or slack if she had it, and use them to light the kindling again the next day. Days wound down when the sun set and people sat around, maybe listening to a wireless if they had one, or singing songs, until they went to bed. In the winter the light would dim around four o'clock and you would hear the birds outside calling to one another, or lifting and falling in murmurations as they settled for the night. Granny would call us to look.

'They're like us,' she would say, 'they like to cuddle together.'

Granny wound us down like the birds, calling out to us, gathering us close under her wings. She fed us goody bread to keep our tummies from waking us in the night. She let us drink tea and she told us stories about ancient kings falling off horses and turning to dust on the road.

She touched us a lot as she knew we needed affection and that we didn't get it at home. She always had a hand on us, patting or softly tracing our skin with her fingertips. She kissed our heads all the time. My granny's body, her arms, her hands, that was where we found some peace. Our tiny empty bones leached what we could out of her warm heart to get us through the week.

She also gave us adventure and taught us boldness and empowerment. She did it in unusual ways, but it worked.

One day she called me close and told me she needed my help with a particular plot. She named it 'Granny and Maureen's Secret Plan'. I swear I almost burst when she included me in it. She pressed her finger to her lips, glanced widely in the direction of my brothers and whispered, 'Don't tell the lads now, this is women's business.'

Women's! I was charmed to be called a woman. I wanted the secret. I would not be telling them lads, not a chance.

I was thrilled to have a secret with my granny. My brothers would have been jealous, but they didn't know and that made it so exciting.

Granny and I plotted to take a half-crown from the basket at Mass. As I've explained, my grandmother wasn't exactly the most pious woman in her community and I think she went to Mass mostly to catch up with neighbours and to avoid the call of the priest to the door. The pennies she put into that basket were ones she could have done with, but I think the hassle of not being seen at Mass was worth the price.

'We have paid into that basket, Maureen, haven't we?' she said, 'Week after week, I put a penny in. And I have done for years.'

I knew this to be true. I was always with her and she always passed that penny to whichever of us whose turn it was and let us drop it in. It made us feel important to do that job.

'Granny, will we get in trouble with the priest?' I asked her in a hush. I leaned into her, enthralled, reached up and touched the chequered skin of her cheek. I rubbed her arm.

'Not at all,' Granny said, 'but we can't tell anyone because everyone will do it and there'll be nothing left in the basket.'

She made sense.

'When the collection basket goes along, *alanna*,' she said, 'you put the penny in, and when you do lift up a half crown and, so nobody sees you, and put it into my pocket.'

She said God wouldn't mind.

'Them rich people who put their half crowns in, it's nothing to them, and sure that priest has plenty of money too,' she said, 'but a penny is all we have this week, and if we put it in, we won't have a drop of milk for the tea. I asked God about it and he let me know that I could take a half crown out – like taking a horse and leaving little chickens.' She was referring to the pictures Irish coins had on them back then. 'We need food, Maureen, and God is going to arrange for us to get it.'

I was in. Granny knew everything about God.

That Sunday, as I sat listening to the tones and indentations of the Latin Mass, those strange wailing sounds that really meant nothing to me, I was excited. The smell of incense in my nostrils, the cold pew under my bare legs, the way the wood on the kneeling bench would dig in to my knees. Mass usually dragged, but this time it flew and before I knew it we were at the last collection. This was it.

Granny had made a list of what we would get in the shop with our half crown and it was long. I squirmed and hopped in my seat. Granny patted my leg to calm me down.

The crucifix loomed above the altar, but Jesus had his face turned away. It was a sign. I could do the job. I had his permission.

Here it came, the basket moved along. Hands passing the handle of it one to the other. The clink of money dropped in, the silence of notes from the front row. As it passed along it sounded like music as the coins scraped together.

It came my way. Everything slowed down. The man beside me passed it to my hands and as he did, the coins all moved together in a wave and settled in the corner. A half crown sat right on top. I placed my penny down, wrapped my hand around that half crown and lifted it out. Granny took the basket from me, I put the coin into her pocket, her hand came in on top of it and squeezed my fingers and that was that. The job was done.

The walk out of Mass led to a relief. My eyes burned a hole in Granny's pocket. I wasn't fearful, I knew God was in our corner. The relief came from the fact that I had done the job well and that we had the money. We walked away richer, the Church was half a crown poorer, but I didn't care.

We went straight to the shop. Granny walked with her head held high, shaking my hand and giving me giddy winks and making kissing sounds at me as we went. She pulled out that list like a town crier as she walked through the door.

With that half crown Granny bought good food – rashers, butter, cigarettes, sugar, tea, chocolate, and an ice-cream wafer each. Mrs Sharkey would cut ice cream from a packet of HB and knock the slab in between two wafers and hand it to you like that. My brothers nearly died, slapping each other's arms as each item landed on the counter and Mrs Sharkey added it to the chit. Michael pinched his own arm to make sure he wasn't dreaming.

I have never felt how I did that day since. The dream of it all. It was, I imagine, how children felt on Christmas morning. A wish coming true.

Granny cooked on an open fire. That was a huge hearth with two concrete hobs on either side, and metal hooks that swung out and across. The fire was built on a high grate in between them. The pots and kettles were black and on chains. She had one pan, with a long handle, that she placed straight onto the coals there. And there was a pot and a kettle that boiled above. She boiled potatoes in their skins, which was how it was done in those days, to be peeled at the table. She made cabbage too.

She held rashers right into the fire on a fork, sitting hunched over on her chair. It had a wobbly back on it so was used just for her. We were warned off sitting on that chair.

Unlike my own house, where there was never enough food or spoons, in Granny's cottage we got our own bowl and our own fork.

She served our dinners out to us with a glass of milk for each and the promise of dessert. We looked at our plates while we prayed over them. *Bless us, O Lord, for these thy gifts …*

Bless my granny. The food filled us, we savoured it and rolled our eyes with the taste of it. Finally, hot milk and sugar and stories by the fire before bed. I felt full, and I wasn't used to a full stomach. I was hot and bothered by it and shifted on my seat. Granny told me to go walk around the room, so I did and it eased off. I was sleepy but I forced myself to stay up to listen to the story. The sooner I went to sleep the sooner Monday morning would come and I just never wanted this wonderful day to end.

Granny lived by the natural law. She knew what was right and what was wrong, and she always did the right thing. She had three grandchildren with bruised faces, skinny legs and empty bellies, and she found ways to keep them going. She saw our empty eyes and broken hearts and knew ways to fill them and mend them.

Those Sunday feasts were repeated from time to time and I believe those Sundays saved us. Those little chinks of magic in a bleak life. But even so, even with such delight, when the time came on Sunday to go to bed, I would feel the twist of anxiety in my insides. Granny would curse the dinner, or lack of, but we both knew what was wrong. So she would rub my tummy and tell me the week would go fast and she would see me on Friday. She would cuddle me in and wipe my tears with her palms and hum a little. Fear twisted me. I knew I would wake up and go straight to hell again. Back to Marty, back to his boots against my bones. Back to the things he wanted from me and the things he made me do.

My granny's cottage was my only experience of childhood. In Marty's I was not a child. I was an animal, keeping my wits about me and trying to survive. Sometimes the stories Granny told would frighten the bejesus out of me, but I never wanted them to end. When they ended it was bed, and with bed came the morning and every morning was another day and the weekend would pass and we would go back to Marty's house. We clung to every word of those stories like we clung to her coat on Monday mornings as she walked us back to school, dreading her leaving us, dreading going back to Green Lane, dreading the week to come.

13

SISTER CECILIA

My school was warm and clean. It's still there, just at the end of Green Lane, up a little hill. They've a new part now. Back then it smelled like bread and sour milk, but in a nice way. I felt relaxed there, so in a strange way I would say I enjoyed school. But I was not paying attention. I was unfriendly and emotionally unable to cope with the politics of little children and the demands of any educator. My lack of participation was largely ignored by the girls in my class and by my teacher, Sister Cecilia.

Sister Cecilia was a tall stern woman in the Presentation Sisters, who wore a black habit with a tight white square wimple around her face. The Presentations were teaching nuns who occupied a convent on Tullow Street and taught in a few schools around. They wore full length black gowns tied with a polished leather belt. When I was really little, I didn't think they had legs. Rosary beads swung from their belts when they walked, with wooden crosses at the end, and they wore flat, black men's shoes. Sister Cecilia was one of the older nuns and she walked with a limp. You don't see those kind of nuns nowadays in Ireland at all. Most of them don't wear habits and it's a dying vocation. But back then, when I was a child, these cloaked women were all over the place. And they were revered by the community. There was only one person who trumped the word of a nun and that was a priest. And there were plenty of those too.

When I was a child, I thought Sister Cecilia's hair might be long under her veil, but I know now it was most likely very short. Nuns took vows of modesty. Her face was severe, square with thick eyebrows and a stern expression permanently set across blue eyes. Most children in our school were terrified of her, but I wasn't. Even now some of my friends will say she was a cold, cruel teacher, who shouted and beat them. I don't remember her shouting at all. She spoke to me in a low voice always. I loved her, not that that means much – my bar for kindness was set so low after all.

But I do believe Sister Cecilia adjusted her manner depending on the child and I think she was softer on me. I was barely there, a small ghost in her classroom and I wonder did she whisper because she was afraid I might fade away in front of her eyes. She was a shining light in that school, for me. She always said, 'Hello, Maureen,' when she passed me, and I remember most times I would loop back and pass her again, to hear my name in her voice once more. My name said in kindness was a comfort, something I didn't hear often. My granny called me *alanna* most times and my mother only called me when she needed something done, a child minded or a hearth cleaned.

From a distance nuns all looked the same, but I knew Sister Cecilia from her funny gait, a polio limp perhaps, under the heavy skirts, and the way she clasped her hands across her stomach.

Sister Cecilia witnessed the change in me over the years as the molestation intensified, as I suffered rape and beatings at home. I had always been a withdrawn child, a child that didn't trust most people, given that I moved from Granny's to Marty's house at three years old, and had only been abused since. But as I got older and he used me how he did, I became like a cornered animal. I was angry and frustrated, and I didn't understand any of it, and I was in constant pain. I never played, and if girls pushed me to join in, I would scream at them or attack them. I shouted at people, anyone who interfered with me, pupils and teachers alike.

I wanted nothing to do with other children; I told them all to leave me alone. I'm not sure why, but I was at the end of my tether I suppose. I didn't want anything of that end of town. I didn't even want to know anyone from there. I wanted to be in Bennekerry and I wanted to live with Granny. It was just who I was. I was hurt and wounded and they'd chastise me and try to drag me in to games to make up numbers and so it was just easier to shout and scream and put them off.

Sister Cecilia had patience for children like me, and so when she was around, I was calmer. She would tell the children to leave me alone, herd me from one task to another with her hand and, whenever I stepped out of line, call me up to the table to talk to me softly about behaving. She never once gave me a beating. I don't know what she saw or thought, but whatever it was, eventually she came to the conclusion that she needed to do something about it. I think she could see that something dark was in my life, something much worse than a simple case of poverty or even neglect. In those days beating children was the norm, and both parents and teachers did it freely, so whatever she noticed – my black bruises, my neglected bones, my upset and agitation when it came to home time – she must have thought it bad enough to try to put a stop to it.

I have to balance the fact that the child I was loved this nun with the fact that the institution she worked for, and the religion she was part of, damaged me so badly. In my view the system she upheld did more damage to Irish people than anything else in history.

14

THE INDIAN DOLL

Just before it all went downhill for me, things were looking up. Sister Cecilia had given me a set of new clothes, including socks and pants from the stores of donations they had taken in from well-off families in Carlow. She brought me to the convent on Tullow Street, and we went through the piles of donated clothing together, looking for something I could have. I loved choosing, I loved the way she held them up against my skinny frame and hummed and hawed, looking for a match to my eyes or skin. It made me feel real and human, the way she looked into my face as she zipped or buttoned the clothes up. She asked me to walk around the room a few times to see the fit of things.

Considering I was last in line for anything at home, despite being the eldest girl, I was often in rags going to school. Raggy bits and bobs with yellow stained socks and worn-out shoes, no wonder she helped me. I was pathetic and any woman would be touched by the state I was in. She was stern but she was not cold-hearted. Perhaps she was also thinking of the reputation of the school itself; to have a pupil so dishevelled wasn't good. Either way 1 was glad of it.

Of course, stripped to my underclothing, trying on the pieces from the pile, Sister Cecilia would have noticed the bruises. I'd imagine the consistency of those marks and the winces 1 made getting in and out of the rig-outs forced her that day to face what was happening to me and to do something about it.

When 1 went home that day with the pile of clothes and told my mother that Sister Cecilia had given them to me, my mother asked me, 'Why did she do that?'

I said 1 didn't know, but 1 held the bundle tight to my chest. I wanted them. There was a skirt and a shirt with a real collar, not like those plastic ones my shirts had, and clean socks.

'She just wanted to give me them,' I said, and 1 told her that I had tried things on so they all fit.

'Does she think you're being neglected?' my mother asked me. It wasn't said in an annoyed way. She genuinely wanted to know.

I shook my head. 1 didn't know what my mother meant. Sister Cecilia was nice to me, that was all 1 thought about it. I didn't have a clue why giving me nice clothes would mean that and 1 didn't know what neglected meant, except that my granny said it sometimes at the dinner table when she got annoyed and made us have more butter on our veg.

'Does she think you get treated badly?' my mother asked me then.

'No, Mammy,' I said. 'She said to me I had stains on my socks.'

'Did she say anything else to you?' My mother was fully engaged with this conversation.

I thought about all the sentences that Sister Cecilia had said when we sat on the floor going through the piles of clothes to find ones that would fit me.

'She said the Murphy girls were always well turned out,' I said.

My mother's eyes went wide. Later I heard her, through the door, telling Marty the whole conversation.

In the week that followed, my life got better. I noticed a little bit more attention my way from my mother. She checked my socks and collars as I went out the door. She gave me lunch for school.

And I noticed it from Marty too. At dinner he wasn't ignoring my plate and putting food on everyone else's first, he was giving me a good portion. And nothing was being taken off me, like it normally was if one of the younger ones cried that they were still hungry – this time they were told to shut up. And Michael was told to empty the bucket and go for milk, even when I was right there.

So right in the middle of that, I chanced my arm.

'Mammy,' I said at the dinner table one night, 'can I save the Daz vouchers up for the Indian doll?'

In those days washing powder came in boxes and most Irish families used Daz powder, which came in a big red box. We used that too in our house, and in Granny's, although Granny used it so sparingly a box would last her a year. When I went back to school that September, all the girls were buzzing about the latest giveaway. If you collected enough vouchers, you could send off and the Daz company would send you back an Indian doll. Lots of girls in my class already had them, but I hadn't seen or touched one. I still wanted one of my own and so Granny and me had been talking about asking my mother to let me. I wanted one so badly it was all I had talked about since the girls across from Granny's house told me they were saving. I don't think before or since I have wanted anything as much as I wanted that doll. Granny was already saving, and she thought I should. She said there was no harm in it. It cost nothing to save those vouchers, she said.

So I asked.

Marty flinched when I did, but my mother said, 'I can't see why not,' and shot a glance at him.

Each box took longer than I hoped to empty, but when it did I cut it up with a big scissors and put the coupon with the others, in an envelope my mother had given me. God knows if it even took me four weeks, but it felt like years. Eventually I had the required amount, and I sent away the envelope with my coupons, all signed on the back, just as the instructions on the box told me to. It was the last real bit of happiness or excitement I ever knew as a child.

I drove everyone mad waiting for that doll. I drove the postman mental. He stopped speaking back to me as I trotted along with his bike on my way to school, talking in hiccups, asking when he would bring me my doll. He brought the post that was given to him, he said enough times.

Then one day I came home from school to our house in Roncalli, and as I came up the drive I saw the door swing open and my mother said, 'Maureen, your package came, the one from Daz–' My God, I blazed past her in the doorway and had it in my hands and torn open before she could finish the sentence and turn around.

She said to Marty later, as he stared at me with a dissatisfied face across the room, that she had never seen anything like the speed of me opening it. I pulled that package open, tore the box. And there she was. Same as the one on the back of the box of Daz, the same one I had been dreaming of all this time, the same doll I really wanted, though in my hands, close up, she seemed smaller. She was the size of my hand, brown like a penny, her hair shiny black and her cheeks pink.

The Indian doll was all mine.

To say that I did not let that doll touch a surface or another hand for the time I had the little thing is no lie. I played with her all day and I slept with her under my top in my armpit. When I ate I held her with one hand under the table or, if I needed both hands, I clasped her with my legs. When I was in school she was in my bag or sometimes under my arm in my cardigan sleeve. She was my thing, my doll. When I was walking home from school I held the doll straight out in front of me so I could see her the whole way.

Her mouth was like a red Cupid's bow. It soon started to wear off from the amount I touched it.

I took that little doll to Granny's and she brought me down to Duckett's Grove with it.

'Now don't you love that doll,' she said.

I did. We went into the forest and my brothers ran ahead.

I started to struggle a little with play around that time, but I tried. I think I was so worn out emotionally from the intensity of the constant rapes, I couldn't find space in my head for imagination. So most times I just played the same scene over and over. With this little doll I dreamed that she was my friend and I lived in Granny's and she lived in Duckett's Grove. I played that we were getting potatoes out of the pit or pulling turnips for a big dinner, where we would eat everything we liked. Sometimes

Granny would play and sometimes we would just sit with my head on her lap, and she would fix my curls behind my ear over and over because they never stayed put. She would tell me stories about old Ireland and the kings that lived there, and how even poor children can be kings at the end of it all.

***

Around that time my brother Michael was sent away to the industrial school. It got even harder to play after that. Not that I had much time left with my childhood anyway.

15

THE SWEET

Not long after that, Sister Cecilia sent for me during sewing and I made my way to her office. I dawdled along the way, thinking it might be an errand she was calling me for and the longer I was gone from class the better. I liked to be alone.

I got to her office slowly and knocked on the door.

'Come in,' she said, and when I did, she said, 'Sit down there, Maureen,' and pointed to one of the big leather armchairs in the corner. They were facing each other and had a table between them. There was a bookshelf beside them and a huge picture of Our Lord Jesus on the wall above it. I sat down and she came out from her desk and sat in the opposite chair. I saw that she had a box of Black Magic in her hand. I'd seen those chocolate boxes behind the counter in Sharkey's shop. Those were luxurious. A red tassel hung from the edge of it. She opened it and inside the Black Magic inserts were gone, but there were other sweets in wrappers filling the box. She rummaged among them and took out a sweet and held it up to me.

It was twice if not three times the size of any sweet I had ever seen before and wrapped in plastic and foil, twisted at each end like a bow. I nearly died.

Sister Cecilia reached over, took my hand and put the sweet into it. I held my palm up with the sweet on it, not moving, the way you might if a butterfly landed there, afraid to move and ruin the magic.

'Is it for me?' I asked.

She nodded.

'To eat?'

She nodded again and I waited for a beat of, maybe, two seconds, asking myself if this could be a dream, then concluding it was not. I unwrapped the sweet and began licking it.

'Maureen,' Sister Cecilia said, 'why don't you play with the other girls?'

I licked the sweet. Why was she asking me that? Had those little bitches told on me? I was annoyed. I licked the sweet again. My mind worked on the problem. Was I in trouble here? But if I was, why would I have this sweet? This did not feel like being in trouble.

Sister Cecilia reached over and unclipped the plastic collar from my shirt. The neckline underneath was filthy. I knew it was from the way she grimaced as she lifted it off. I wore that shirt day in and day out and it was rarely washed. I only had the one shirt, and the one she had given me the day before was in my mother's room where she had put them.

'Maureen, where are the clothes I gave you?' she said.

I licked my sweet.

'Maureen, is there something you should tell me?' she said.

93

She was speaking in a kind voice, but there was something in her tone then that stopped me licking my sweet and I wrapped it back up in the plastic and curled my fingers around it. I was encouraged to at least consider replying to her, but I thought twice about it and decided to say nothing.

Her hand went into the box again and this time she pulled out a flat wrapped sweet that looked like a penny. I wondered how long I could draw this conversation out and maybe I would get enough sweets for me and Paddy and Granny.

'Maureen,' Sister Cecilia said, 'do you know what we think?'

I looked around the room. Who was 'we'?

'Maureen,' she said, 'we think someone is being very, very bad, and we think that person is doing bad things and we think they do them to you.'

My mind raced away from the sweets straight to Marty. Was she talking about him? I looked around the room again. What was this? Who was 'we'? Who knew what and how did they know? I had never told anyone about what Marty was doing. He had warned me not to or he would kill me and feed me to the pigs. He said he would throw me in with my father. I didn't want to be eaten by pigs, with their flat teeth and huge tongues. I didn't want to be cold and wrapped in blankets underground like my father was.

I unwrapped a corner of my sweet and licked it.

She wanted an answer, but I couldn't tell her. I considered telling her I had a terrible pain. I could howl as well and clutch my belly, that might work. Maybe they'd bring me back to hospital. Without thinking I put the sweet all the way into my mouth and bit into it. My mouth filled with a heavenly mush of chocolate and caramel.

Sister Cecilia pushed her wimple back a little, shook her head and adjusted how she was sitting so she could put her hand out to me.

'I think it would be a good idea if you could tell us who is hurting you this way,' she said.

I looked around again and caught the eye of the Sacred Heart in the corner of the room. I thought that maybe this 'we' was Sister Cecilia and them – Jesus, God, the saints. I mean nuns were holy and could speak straight to God. If God had told her, well the cat was out of the bag.

My mouth was full. I slurped and chewed and swished my tongue around the inside of my cheeks. I slurped again and licked the corner of my lip where chocolate dribbled out.

I didn't think I should tell. This could be a con. Maybe she knew nothing.

'What would make you happy in life, Maureen?' she asked me then.

I knew the answer to that. I slurped and spoke through the chocolate. 'Liv – ith – ranny,' I said, but it was unintelligible, so I chewed and slurped and swallowed and said it again, 'Living with my granny.'

'Oh?' Sister Cecilia said. 'The one in Bennekerry?'

I nodded.

'Could she keep you, Maureen?' she said. 'Has she the money do you think?'

I nodded firmly. I couldn't tell Sister Cecilia about the half crowns, although it seemed she knew everything about me already, so I said, 'Granny has chickens,' as if that was the key to it, 'and potatoes in a pit.' Me and Granny would be just fine.

Sister Cecilia nodded then and sat back. I jumped to the conclusion that this was now a plan. Suddenly there was an escape route from Marty, and Sister Cecilia was lighting the way to it. I thought, genuinely, that she was going to tell Granny to keep me and that would be that. I have never felt relief like it.

Sister Cecilia had such a pleasant face on, perhaps she too thought that right then. She said, 'If you did live with Granny, well ...', she sat forward again and pushed her wimple back a little again, 'you'd still have to tell me who is hurting you, Maureen. That's very important.'

To be honest the idea of living with Granny and never going back to Marty's house had me floating. I felt so light. I could almost feel Granny's arms around me, the warmth of her cottage stretching all the way to that office in school. I could have Granny all to myself and sleep in her bed every single night. I could choose left side or right side and hold any hand I wanted and I could go and do the messages for her all by myself.

For that, I would have told Sister Cecilia anything she wanted to know.

So when she said, 'Tell me, Maureen,' that one last time – I did.

I told her about all the babies my mother had, and the buckets of wee and my socks, and the way Marty kicked and punched me and my brothers every day. I kept going, told her about the coffee and the aunts and the way Shay fought him. I told her about Granny Quinn telling on me, and the way my mother went out to work all day and Marty didn't.

She sat and listened, but I knew this wasn't the information she wanted. I could tell by her face.

So I told on him. I told on Marty. I sat there in that room with a chocolate mouth and an open heart and talked about it. I told her about the milking, and Marty's braces and threats, and the way he pushed on me. I told her how he hurt my neck with his arm when he lay on me and the way I got pains in my tummy and bum. I told her how I thought my legs would pop out because he pushed on me so hard.

She flinched when I said that. I shut up.

Sister Cecilia took a moment. She was pale and I saw her swallow. I thought suddenly to myself that maybe I had misunderstood the question.

'Maureen,' she said, and she put a hand on my shoulder and squeezed it, 'I want you to go to the hall, not back to class, go to the hall and find a book and read it. Good girl now, I will come to get you in a minute.'

She opened the door and I walked through it, half wishing I could reverse the entire meeting and keep my secrets. I felt as though I had signed my own death warrant. With that burden shared the school suddenly looked unfamiliar, the halls looked longer and strange to me. I went out of her office and down the hall and did as I was told.

My secret was out and something in the way Sister Cecilia looked at me as I went told me this wasn't as simple as going home with Granny after all.

16

THE PRIEST

I sat beside the radiator in the hall and held a book in my hand, but it may as well have been upside down for all I was reading it. I loved books, but that day my thoughts were going too fast to look at it. The radiator I sat against warmed through my cardigan and top and soothed my sore back. I picked up another book and didn't read that either. I was watching the window.

I heard the sound of a nun swish by.

I put the current book on my lap and picked up another book, glancing up to see the parish priest out the window – Father Lawlor. He was a squat man with a dark five o'clock shadow and wiry wavy hair that he wore greased against his head. His thick neck was forced into a black shirt with the white starched wraparound collar that gave him the keys to the universe. That collar made Lawlor the most powerful man in our town.

Lawlor's mouth was always turned down in a permanent sneer and he wore, with his shirt, a long black cassock under which his shoes showed, gleaming and polished. He wore a black cover over his shoulders.

I watched out the window and saw that he was greeted by Sister Cecilia. She bowed a little and ushered him through the door. I heard her say, 'Thank you for coming, Father,' and her face wasn't soft like it had been in the office. It was firm and set in a scowl, and her mouth was a straight line. She unnerved me. They walked right by me, briskly, and Sister Cecilia didn't look at me and neither did the priest. That unnerved me even more. The door of her office shut behind them with a click.

I thought about going back to the class and wondered if the rules of confession applied to nuns – maybe she couldn't tell anyone, but I knew that was a silly thing to think. I knew she was in that office telling the priest what I had said. I had no idea what was to come of this.

I took another book down, flipped through it and put it back. I did that over and over again with the same book until I heard the office door open again and Sister Cecilia called my name. She appeared then and beckoned to me. Her face had no colour. She was pale. Everything suddenly seemed pale, like the saturation in a photograph had been lowered.

I was terrified of the parish priest. He never shut up about hell and demons and burning forever if you had impure thoughts. I knew the pain of burning – I'd once grabbed a hot saucepan without a cloth and it hurt me badly for weeks. Impure thoughts were how you ended up in the fires of hell, according to this man, but what were those? How would I know what thoughts were good and what were bad? He said we were all sinners. We would all be going there, he said. I didn't want to go to hell.

I imagined as I walked towards it that the office would open up and I would fall straight into the fires there and then. What powers did this parish priest have exactly? I was about to find out.

When I walked in Sister Cecilia was at her desk writing something on a piece of paper and the parish priest was standing looking at her do it.

He turned to me. 'Miss Sullivan,' he said, 'the sister is writing a note for your mother.'

I looked at the nun. What was she doing that for? Oh, I knew, maybe it was a note to say I was going home to Granny's. Sister Cecilia folded the paper into a brown envelope and closed it. She wrote on the front of it. I was lightheaded with joy, thinking I knew what it said inside. I was going to live at Granny's, it had to be that.

The priest said, 'Listen now, you run home and give that note only to your mother, nobody else, do you hear me?'

I nodded. They meant Marty when they said nobody else, I knew that. I wouldn't let him near it. I'd eat it if I had to. He would stop me going to Granny's. He would kill me and feed me to the pigs if he knew I told on him.

I held the letter in two hands and looked at the way Sister Cecilia had written my mother's name – Mrs Murphy – all joined up together with a little curl on the M's. That letter really meant the world to me. I believed it was my saving grace, my royal pardon.

I did what I was told, clutching the letter in two hands pressed against my ribs the whole way home. I stood there until my mother came in from the back and then I handed it to her solemnly. She asked me what was in it, but I shrugged. I knew my mother found reading difficult, but I didn't want to jump the gun. I wanted to see what they said when she did.

'I hope you're not in trouble, Maureen,' she said, opening it, pulling the envelope apart awkwardly and taking out the note.

'I amn't,' I said.

When I saw the look that overtook her face as she started to read slowly, silently mouthing the words out with her breath as she did, I started to wish I had never told. I could have just sat there eating sweet after sweet and said nothing.

A sharp intake of breath from my mother made me jump. It was game over, I knew it. The cat was out of the bag. I knew immediately from the way my mother rushed around to get her coat and her bag that the note had nothing in it about living with Granny. She didn't look at me or speak to me and a surging twist of anxiety gripped my whole body.

What was in that letter?

My mother told me sharply to go straight back to school. She said she needed to find someone to mind the babies and when she did, she would come down.

So I went back, and I sat outside Sister Cecilia's office as I had been instructed. I wanted to take it all back. Pandora's box was wide open. All the evils of this world were swarming in the air around me and I could feel them.

My mother arrived, red-faced and flustered. My mind turned into a rolling slot machine of possibilities of how this was going to go. Maybe I should say I made it up or say I was sorry. Maybe I should run to Granny's right now and hide in the potato pit until they all stopped looking for me. Then I thought twice about that – Marty might kill Granny. I almost retched at the visual image in my mind of him throwing her across the cottage the way he threw me. She would break. What had I done?

My mother came in the door of the school and saw me. 'Why are you not in class?' she asked but didn't wait for me to answer. As she went by me, she turned and said, 'Oh Maureen, what have you done?' She knocked on the office door and disappeared through it.

What had I done?

***

About five minutes later the door opened again, but this time the parish priest came out of it and flew by me with his cassock flying behind him. He paused just a moment in his stride as he passed me, but I didn't look up and he didn't stop. He swooped out the door and down the drive, skirts and cloak flying behind him. He looked so angry and he terrified me.

I studied the walls, found animals in the swirls of the lino floor and stared out the window. I listened to the sounds of the school; girls were singing in the distance and I hummed along. Two girls, clearly on an errand, passed and saw me and whispered to each other. Did everyone know?

Sister Cecilia came out to get me. I saw when I went in that my mother had been crying. Her face was blotchy and her eyes were red and watery and she was blowing her nose. I could not understand that part back then – my mother in tears made no sense.

Now I think she was crying with the shame of it. I don't know what was said to her, but I imagine that she sat down in that office with the parish priest and nun and was told that her daughter had accused her husband of sexual abuse. I don't know if they'd have gone softly on that with her or told her outright, but I think they told her. That kind of family secret is rarely exposed and perhaps she blamed herself for what had been happening, that she turned a blind eye to it. She had brought her three children into that house after all and trapped us there to be treated no better than animals.

My mother was cut from a different cloth than Granny Sullivan. My grandmother was independent, knew her own mind and was a fighter. My mother was not. But in fairness to her, this country of ours had no time for women's rights, certainly not then. The family was enshrined in the new constitution, one that our government took advice on from the Church itself when writing it, and the man was the head of the family and that was that. Above everything, above safety, happiness and human rights, the family unit was cherished most of all. So how can I blame my mother for any of it, when everything was set against her from the start?

I do believe Mary Quinn did her best, both as Mrs Sullivan and Mrs Murphy. I know I cast my father as an angel because I never knew him and from how my granny and uncle spoke of him in their stories, but who knows for sure? Men were supreme and women were not in Ireland in those days. I think my mother turned a blind eye because she told herself she was wrong about things, or she felt that if she interfered it would make things worse for us. Or she worried he would make her give us up – there are too many stories of that happening in second marriages to ignore.

But as a twelve-year-old child, in that moment, I could not work out what on earth she was crying for. I saw things as children do, in simple terms.

When I went into the office, I naturally sidled in beside her and she placed her arm around my shoulders. I was surprised by it, as it is the only time I can remember my mother touching me in a protective way.

She whispered, 'Sister needs a word with us, girl.'

Sister Cecilia stood behind her desk. The soft voice that she had spoken to me with earlier, the one she eased the information out of me so well with, was gone. She spoke with firm authority, said I was to go home and not leave my mother's side this evening. She told my mother not to leave me alone. My mother agreed, nodded profusely, said, 'Yes, Sister, of course.'

Sister Cecilia's tone unnerved me, but perhaps she was speaking that way for my mother's benefit, not mine. It was – looking back – a serious situation. But at that time I felt a sense of suddenly being judged that has never left me. I felt on trial, and in a way I was. I would be sentenced in the morning.

The nun said again, 'Maureen, remember what I am saying to you. Do not leave your mother's side tonight and we will see you in the morning.'

I stared at the crucifix on the wall. Jesus was looking away again. I stared and stared, but he didn't meet my eyes at all.

17

THE SOLUTION

As we went home, sticking to the footpath together with my mother's feet moving so fast I had to trot to keep up, she said to me, 'Maureen, don't say nothing to no one right now, but you are going to go to a new school, alright?'

I was unimpressed with this solution, but anyway I didn't have anyone to tell except Paddy. So I agreed. What good was this idea? A new school wouldn't solve anything. My trouble wasn't even with school. I liked school. It was a place where Marty Murphy wasn't. He would get me as soon as I got home from the new place anyway, that was for sure. He always did. It was a load of rubbish. A new school was solving nothing.

It all seemed so pointless. I had told my secrets and all I got was a new school. Sister Cecilia was what I liked about my school and I liked the girls because I knew them, even though I shouted at them and attacked them. I liked that they knew already to leave me alone. I liked the walk to school too. It was a short walk and didn't hurt my hips too much. What good was a new one to me at all?

Then I stopped walking because I had had a thought. What if the new school was in Bennekerry? Perhaps that was what Sister Cecilia was planning. Maybe she didn't want to hurt my mother's feelings by saying I wanted to live with Granny, so if she moved me up to that school it would just make sense to go home across the way, instead of three miles back to Carlow. That must be it. It had to be. My world felt bright. I said a little prayer of thanks to God.

'Maureen, come on,' my mother called over her shoulder. I caught up with her just before she crossed the road.

***

At the back of Roncalli Place, at that time, was a field. It was a sort of waste ground that would eventually have houses on it, but back then it served as a playground for children and somewhere for people to take a walk. In the evenings when my mother came in from work, she would sometimes send me out for a walk if she could see Marty was agitated. It was like therapy. The cool evening air of dusk would soothe my skin and I could disappear into the Carlow twilight and focus on the small things – the sounds of the last children out playing, the birds, the wind. Dogs barking in the distance. All of those things sounded the same at Granny's.

I used to walk around and around that field. If Marty had harmed me that day it was soothing to take slow steps and move through the pain. I could rub my tummy in circular motions and breathe. I took a walk that night. I asked if I could go and was instructed by my mother to speak to nobody and come back before Marty got home from wherever he was that evening.

Until the next morning I had absolutely no idea that it would be my last walk around that field, my last night in Roncalli Place, the last time I would mind the younger ones and help my mother, the last time I would eat there and the last time I would make Marty Murphy his beloved cup of coffee.

My mother paid a lot of attention to me that night. She kept me in the kitchen with her and sent one of the others instead when Marty called my name. She kept finding reasons to keep me busy: 'Maureen, wash that pot. Maureen, rock the pram. Maureen, sweep there, and there. Good girl.'

I'll admit to you now that I never had such attention from my mother before and it was lovely. She was fully focused on me. Normally she was too busy, too distracted with her chores and her younger children to pay attention to the oldest ones. But not this night. This night it was as if ... well it *was* our last night and she knew it, even if I didn't.

At the dinner table she sat beside me. I kept looking up at her face as we ate, and at one point she passed me a piece of her bread. Then, out of nowhere, she reached over and fixed a stray curl back behind my ear.

'You've lovely hair,' she said, 'you don't get that hair from me.'

I remember looking at her dark curly hair. Over the years and babies it got shorter and shorter, but it was still beautiful. As a child I always wanted my mother's hair. I didn't recognise my own blonde wavy hair in anyone I knew. Now I know I got my hair from my dad's side. That is what she was referring to that night. In the few hours we had left together, she was reminding me, and herself perhaps, that I was John L. Sullivan's daughter.

That night, before I went to bed, my mother called me upstairs and we went through my things. She folded each one into a small pile at the end of her bed. Then she went to the other side of the room and pulled a small brown case from behind the bed and opened it. We packed all of those things I owned into it. I was existing on a roller coaster, thinking I was going to Granny's, thinking I wasn't, thinking I was again. When she packed the case, I became fully certain of it. I was definitely going to Bennekerry. Why else would I need my stuff?

You see, I had no real understanding of life outside that little patch of Carlow where Duckett's Grove was at one end, our house was at the other, and Granny's somewhere in between. The only nuns I knew were in my town or the few in the hospital I had met. So packing a bag was something I could only associate with the few times we went to Granny's in the summer for longer. I could never have imagined the life that was coming for me. Not in a million years.

My mother pressed her hand on my forehead when I went to bed that night and she whispered not to get up until she came to get me in the morning. My hand stayed pressed on where her hand had been as I started to drift into sleep. I came awake again when I heard Marty's gammy feet on the stairs and that shuffle along the landing. I heard him stop by the kids' room and I felt the weight of his stare through the doorway.

Then I heard my mother. She came to the bottom of the stairs.

'Is there anything I can get you now before you go to bed?' she called up.

There was a pause.

'No, nothing,' Marty said back to her, and he moved away from my door and I heard the springs of his own bed groan.

My mother worked downstairs as always that night. I could hear the sounds of her moving around, sweeping, washing the few plates and cups. I heard the back door go, open and closed, as she brought the slops outside for the offal man to collect – we had no pigs in Roncalli Place – and then she brought in coal and wood.

She kept coming halfway up the stairs, just far enough perhaps that she could see the shapes in the beds they belonged in, to make sure I was okay.

***

I slept that night and woke earlier than everyone else, but I remembered what my mother had said and so I stayed there until she came around the door and whispered for me to get up.

18

THE PENCIL CASE

I was given the plan.

Sister Cecilia used her soft voice, and she pushed her wimple back as she spoke to me. 'Maureen, you're going to a lovely new school. Do you understand?'

I nodded.

Sister Cecilia said, 'Mam agrees that it's the best thing, alright?'

I nodded. I was holding myself together. My mother was still holding my hand and she squeezed it.

'How do you feel about that, Maureen?'

I was on my guard.

'What school is it?' I said. I wanted all of the information.

'It's a lovely school in New Ross,' Sister Cecilia said, as if I had one clue as to where or what New Ross was, 'in Wexford.' I'd heard of Wexford.

'What's wrong with this school?' I said. I tried to make the connection.

'Well,' Sister Cecilia knew why I was asking, 'it's a school where you live. You will sleep there with all the other children who go there.'

Not Granny's. Not Bennekerry.

My mother shook my hand in hers. 'It's a lovely school, Maureen,' she said, red in the face, signing my life away without knowing it. The desire to fix this problem, something she knew now for sure, conflicted, I'd imagine, with the loss of help – I did a lot for my mother – and because she did love me. The nuns were authority and my mother didn't stand up for herself, let alone anyone else. She was no rebel, as I have said before. She took their instruction.

I do wonder exactly what Sister Cecilia had told her or told the parish priest. I'm sure the information was passed in hints and well-worded code. But then I think, what could my mother have done? There was no divorce, and women were considered the property of their husbands. She was as stuck as I was.

My mother and Sister Cecilia took one of my hands each and I was taken outside the school right then and there.

'Now, Maureen, there is a man on the way to bring you down,' Sister Cecilia said.

My mother made a strange movement then, like a bolt, and she raised her hand and for a minute I thought she was going to object to all of this. Maybe she was, but then all she said was, 'Sister, I'm sorry, how long till she goes?'

'Well, the lift will be here in a minute, Mrs Murphy,' Sister Cecilia said.

'I'll be back in one minute,' she said, 'don't let her go till I'm back,' and she raced away, walking briskly down the drive from the school to where the town lay. I watched her.

While we waited Sister Cecilia suggested we say a decade of the Rosary, and so we did.

Blessedarethefruitsofthywombjesus ...

I never understood any of the words I was saying; it was like chanting.

We finished the decade. Sister Cecilia thought about starting a new one, but then she remembered she had to show me the bag she had with my new books inside. She had three books or maybe four, all covered in flowery wallpaper like most people did in those days, well, people with wallpaper anyway. I loved the look of those new books, and the smell of them and the feel of them in my hands as she handed them to me. She had put my name inside in the corner. This was something.

Sister Cecilia took my schoolbag and told me my mother would bring it home, as I didn't need one in the new place, since I would live there too.

Then my mother came back, pushing herself up the hill, clearly relieved I was still there. She caught her breath back quickly – women in those days were fit from walking and from work. She handed me a brown bag. I retrieved out of it a pencil case, some pencils and a rubber and topper, and some copy books.

'Thank you, Mammy,' I said, and I meant it. These were things that farmer's daughters brought in and set on their desks proudly. These weren't things that I'd ever had or dreamed of having.

That was something my mother had done before, when I was going to the hospital and she bought me a new nightdress. She did have pride and it presented itself whenever her children might be judged. That's a sort of love, isn't it? My nightdress, my name on the Christmas party form, this pencil case, all showed that my mother didn't want me to be judged. She didn't want to be judged either.

The pencil case was a wooden box with a roll-top mechanism, like a garage door, where the lid rolls into itself to open. There was a small, raised flower, painted blue, in the corner. I put the pencils inside it. They would need a sharpener.

I pushed the pencil case open and shut it over and over. It was beautiful.

We waited.

Then I saw the black roof of a van slow down by the gate.

'Tell Granny where to collect me on Friday,' I said to my mother, wondering in that moment how long the walk was from the new school.

They both gasped, and Sister Cecilia shook her head very definitely with a frown.

'Maureen,' she said quite sternly, 'you'll be staying at the new school on weekends too, so don't be thinking ahead. If you don't like it, you can come back.'

I wrinkled up my nose and started to shake my head. I could not live without my granny.

Sister Cecilia's mouth went into a hard line. 'Maureen,' she said, sensing my resistance and wagging a finger at me, 'we have made arrangements. You'll go down to this new school and get a good education and you can come back to us all an educated girl. Won't that be wonderful?'

It would, I supposed. My mother was smiling so widely when Sister Cecilia said that. She really seemed to want me to go to the new school.

'Now, Maureen,' my mother said. She always said that when she was pleased. I thought to myself that there must be something special in this. I was getting new books and pencil cases and lifts in vans.

I said, 'Thank you,' to Sister Cecilia. I really meant it – the look on my mother's face was blowing my mind. If my mother was this delighted, it must be really something.

**

The black van pulled up the drive and stopped just before us. A man hopped out of the cab and said a cheery 'Good morning' to me and my mother, and a more reserved 'Sister' to Sister Cecilia.

My mother started crying.

'I'll miss you, Maureen,' she said. Her voice was wobbling, but she didn't pull me in for a hug or give me a kiss. In fact, I don't think I ever had either from my mother. Years of abuse and depression kept us to ourselves even then, as we said as heartfelt a goodbye as either of us could muster, as damaged as we were.

The van driver opened the passenger door and said, 'Will it be yourself?' to me, which I liked. I climbed in and he popped my suitcase beneath me. He went to take the pencil case, but I hung on tight.

'I'll leave that with you so,' he said and winked at me.

He spoke to Sister Cecilia for a minute as me and my mother stared at one another through the glass. She said, 'Be good' a few times and I said, 'I will.'

As the van pulled away, I waved at my mother, 'Be good,

Maureen,' she called after the van, over and over, and I watched her until we rounded the corner, her faraway mouth still moving as I drove away.

19

ST MARY'S

I sat in the front seat of the black laundry van as it drove across to Wexford. It was a scenic drive and he pointed out various bits and bobs to me as we went.

'There's horses for you now,' he said.

I looked. He wasn't wrong.

There was no motorway then, and the journey took hours along two-lane roads that sometimes ran along the dark brown Barrow river. Houses passed us in flashes. I saw people walking, men with their caps on, women with their scarves. Familiar Irish scenes.

I saw babies in prams outside doorways, and women pinning washing onto lines. I saw men opening huge gates to let tractors through and onto the road. I saw little dogs in windows, and cats on rooftops. I looked out the window at the clouds in the sky and found faces and animals in them.

The driver would pull in along our way, stopping outside garda stations and institutions and small guesthouses, collecting huge pregnant bags of laundry that made him waddle like a penguin as he carried them and stuffed them into the back. I watched him carry the laundry in the mirror beside my window. I found it amusing to see him peer over the top of the bags. Every time we would pull in, he would say, 'Stay there for a minute.'

He had bags to return, smaller, neater, full of folded uniforms and pressed sheets and pillowcases. I could smell the freshness in the cab. It was lovely.

He would make those exchanges in places along the way, and every time he stopped, he would ask me, 'Do you want to go to the toilet?' And I would shake my head even though towards the end of the journey I did.

I was mildly afraid of him. Even though he was nice to me, I was nervous. I remember sitting in the cab, pushing the roll-top on my pencil case back and forward with my fingertip for the entire journey. At one point the driver said, 'You love that pencil case, don't you?'

When he spoke to me, I pushed it back and forth more quickly. By the time we got to New Ross my fingertip was red.

***

I saw a sign that said New Ross – the driver pointed it out – and not long after we passed really high stone walls and at the end of them, we pulled in under an archway into a small yard. I knew it was the last stop because the driver didn't tell me to stay there for a minute or ask if I needed the toilet. Back outside the archway there were cottages on the other side of the road and a shop. The journey had taken us so long, I knew I was miles and miles from home.

The driver hopped out and instead of going to the back of the van, he walked around the front and opened my door and physically lifted me under the arms placing me square on the ground. He lifted my suitcase out and put it at my feet.

'Now,' he said.

St Mary's Convent, New Ross, loomed up from the yard where we stood. It is still there, a huge grey stone building, built in the Victorian Gothic style of churches and cathedrals, put together by the Good Shepherd order in the late 1800s as an asylum for fallen women. The idea of Magdalene asylums originally was to retrain women working in prostitution as domestics, as a way to get them off the streets and away from danger and disease. But these refuges soon became another sort of place, a storehouse for women who needed to be put away. There were no babies in New Ross and no pregnant women when I arrived. From what I know now, it was a place to put 'difficult' inmates from other laundries, or promiscuous girls.

I've been back there as an adult, so my memory might be confused, but I do think the driver deposited me in the little yard through two gates where he also deposited the laundry bags. There was a pump there, and low-lying buildings – I think painted cream – wrapped around enclosing it entirely, joined at one side to the huge granite convent with doors through which two nuns suddenly appeared.

They crossed to us. They practically ran. I noticed they didn't dress like Sister Cecilia or the sisters in the Carlow convent, but I knew they were nuns. They wore loose cream habits to their feet, and white wimples covered with black veils that fell over their shoulders. Of the two who came towards us, one was tall and skinny, and the other was plump and short.

I called out 'Hello' and waved at them. I was ignored and they greeted the driver.

'Thank you, Mister,' they said and directed him to deposit his bags in the side door, which he began to do as I waited there. I noticed thin grey arms extending from the doorway to take the heavy bags, slumping every time he let go. I stared.

What was this place?

I considered telling them I'd just go back to Carlow now. Sister Cecilia had said I could if I didn't like it, but I could smell something cooking. I need the loo badly and so I thought I'd just stay the one night.

The driver came back to the van, checking around where I was sitting to make sure nothing was dropped or left, and closed the door. That was that, then.

Neither of the nuns looked me in the eye or spoke to me. But the tall one reached down and took a hold of my pencil case. I held on to it. She pulled and I pulled back.

'It's mine,' I said. 'My mammy gave it me,' I told her.

She held it and twisted it and I had to twist it back to keep it in my hand. The driver coughed and shuffled a bit on his feet, clearly uncomfortable with this silent attack on the little child he had brought all the way here with his laundry round.

'No,' I said, 'my mammy gave it me, it's my pencil–' and it was gone. She had it up and away and into her pocket.

I never saw my lovely pencil case again.

20

FRANCES

I was taken to the office then, by the arm. The smaller plump nun had me in a grip above the elbow, like you might be held by a policeman. She was walking faster than me and I ended up almost sideways, trotting as fast as I could so as not to fall over.

I don't know which part of the building I was in, but it was close to the laundry because I could smell and hear it. There were painted walls, and lino on the floor.

The tall nun, whose pocket held my pencil case, sat down at the desk in the office. She bent first, opened a bottom drawer and slid something in. I knew it was my pencil case. I muttered, 'My mammy gave it me.'

The nun opened a large book, full of lines of writing, and she scanned it first before putting on a pair of small wire-framed glasses that made her eyes look twice the size. She looked up at me over them, scanned me from top to bottom and then back at the page in front of her.

She sighed, 'Will we call you Frances?' and looked at me expectantly.

'Oh, I'm called Maureen,' I corrected her. I stared at the desk where I knew my pencil case was. Why had she taken it? Maybe for safekeeping until I started school.

'Frances will be your name here in Saint Mary's,' the nun said. 'That's how we do things,' and she wrote a long line of joined-up writing into her ledger. I think now she wrote me as a penitent into that book. Maureen Sullivan was never mentioned again in my life for years.

I didn't want to be called Frances, but I wasn't given much choice. I liked my name, my granny told me it was a name that meant little Mary, the same name as Our Blessed Lady. And my mother's name was Mary, so I cherished that. Maureen was my name and I wanted to keep it. If they changed it how would anyone know me?

But then I remembered that Sister Cecilia had another name too, one that some of the girls from school had seen when she dropped a letter one day, and for a moment I wondered was I now a nun too? I hoped not.

For years I couldn't figure out why our names were changed in the Magdalene laundries. What reason had they? A number would have made more sense to me if they wanted us to be nothing and nobody. But a number is a way to trace us, and it would have been unique. It would have to be remembered and displayed somewhere. By changing our names they made sure, not that we struggled on the inside, but that on the outside we had no way to identify or find each other. And how could we stand as a witness to what went on there if there was nothing to say we had been there at all? We didn't exist.

When the nun was finished writing in her book, she stood up and brought me - again by the elbow - down the hall to where I could hear swishing machine sounds and the hum of something.

She pushed the door open and my eyes were met with the stares of about forty others. I tried to back away, to wriggle out of her grasp and make a run for it. But the nun held on tight and moved me forward into the steam-filled room full of standing dead women.

I had never seen a Magdalene laundry. I could not believe my eyes.

**

There were women everywhere. It looked so strange to me initially because they were all dressed in the same outfit - a grey dress and cardigan - and they all had the same short, bobbed hair. Some of them had a clip in it. One or two of them had shaven heads. That was the treatment, in those days, for lice. The women were all ages; some were elderly and some were a bit younger than that, but none were as young as me. Every one of them was thin and not one of them smiled.

There were maybe forty of them, at least that. They all looked at me, and some of them had open mouths, some of them were frowning. I expected them to say hello, but not one of them spoke. I wondered were they nuns, but my gut said no. Why would nuns have rolled-up sleeves and red hands from working? That made no sense. Then something struck me - hadn't Sister Cecilia told me I would sleep at school? Two women were folding a blanket and I thought I was being given a tour and this was where all the bed linen was being washed. I wasn't sure why they wanted me to see it, but I supposed that was helpful in some way. They were clearly proud of it, the way they were telling me all about the machines and how they worked, and telling me the system they used to get the washing done in good time. I nodded along.

'This is the machine for pressing, the calendar,' the plump nun said, and she laid a smooth white hand on the handle of a huge machine that had wheels that rolled a large barrel along a table. A woman stepped out of her way to let her show me the thing. I could see sweat on that woman, her upper lip was wet, her underarms had stained grey dark and she was heaving for breath.

The nun moved me on, to where the women were folding the sheets. She ran through that system with me too. 'End to end, fold, fold,' she said.

She stopped at a mangle, a machine where wet blankets were fed through and wrung over and over until they were almost dry.

'Turn the handle,' the nun said, 'give it a good pull down and turn it.'

I could barely reach the handle to pull it down, and so the nun beckoned one of the women to pull it down for me, rather than pulling it herself. Then I pushed it up and over, lifting off my feet each time with the momentum. Did they want me to have a go and stop? But nobody told me to stop.

The laundry was bright, due to the large Gothic windows that poured sunlight in on top of the workers, glittering through the steam and sparkling on the women's faces. The floor was painted concrete, grey, the walls were cream, I think, and there were all sorts of pulley systems and ropes criss-crossing the ceiling and walls above my head. Tubs and buckets and vats and baskets were around the walls. Washing machines stood rattling against the back wall. And everything smelled clean.

It was so hot in there it was stifling. I started to gasp a little and tried to cool myself down by slipping my school cardigan off my shoulders to let the tops of my arms breathe. My legs were sticking together.

All of a sudden there was an elderly woman approaching, in the same grey uniform as the others, with the same bobbed hair, but she was very old, probably as old as my granny. Her skin was thin and papery and clung to her bones in parts. It hung off her chin in two wattles, and she was toothless except for one long middle tooth that creased into her bottom lip. She bent down to me and got too close. I was afraid of her. She was like the walking dead. I stopped turning the handle.

'Back to work, Annie,' the nun said to her. Annie glanced at her but ignored her. Her eyes were wide as can be and she was making a cooing sound, as though I were a baby or a kitten she had found. She seemed a little drunk and she reached out to take my hand, but I whipped it back behind me.

'Hello, pet,' Annie said, and touched my cheek with a tsk tsk noise she made with her lips against her one tooth.

Then the nun roared at her, so loudly I jumped, 'Annie! Enough!' And I watched the nun raise a hand to her and whack the old lady hard on the shoulder. It didn't seem to bother Annie much. She just turned and shuffled off.

I was horrified. What kind of place was this where nuns were angry mothers and elderly women were chastised and hit like children?

I wanted to go over to where the children were and get out of this place. I was frightened of these women's gaunt faces and stares. Where were my classmates? My new friends? I wanted them to see my pencil case and think I was a farmer's daughter. What was going on?

All I could see were sad grey women, washing and scrubbing, and nobody was speaking, not one word between them.

***

A younger woman in her forties suddenly appeared, and she was introduced to me as the 'trustee'. She was dressed the same as the other women, but she had longer hair and she wasn't frazzled and sweating like they were. I wondered was this my teacher to take me to school.

'My name is Emily,' she said. The nun told her my name was Frances. I shook my head. 'It's Maureen,' I said.

'Hello, Frances,' Emily said, and I knew immediately who she was in cahoots with. But I just decided to ignore it. My new name jarred so badly in my ear. I didn't know what a trustee was anyway, but I soon came to use it as you would 'warden'. That was what Miss Emily seemed to be, anyway.

At that point Emily took my arm and brought me back out along the corridor again, past the door I had come in and round a corner to where there were steps down and the ceiling got lower. This is how I remember it anyway. We went through a door and in front of us was a low, long corridor with no windows. The old fluorescent lights barely reached into the corners. It was a tunnel, but I wouldn't know what it would come to mean for me, that place. I didn't know I would become the girl in the tunnel, and that people outside the convent would come to whisper about me, as though I were a myth or a ghost. That hidden corridor for a hidden girl meant nothing at that point.

At the other end of the tunnel, Emily opened a door to what was clearly a school. I could hear the familiar sounds of children and I heaved a sigh of relief. My mistake was righted. I was going to school here. There were classes and children and a yard.

Thanks be to God.

I hoped I would never see that laundry again and wondered would I get my pencil case back soon.

21

ST AIDAN'S

I could hear faint voices instructing children behind one door we passed, and noises of moving furniture from another. A door opened and closed. Emily pulled me by all of them to a staircase at the end with a turned banister, where a white stone saint stood in a niche built for it. There was another one at the top as we went up. She brought me along to double doors that revealed a dormitory beyond with beds lined up against the wall exactly as you'd imagine, each with a pillow and blankets folded neatly under and a white sheet doubled down over the top.

Beside each bed was a small wooden locker. There was nothing else there. Miss Emily showed me the bathroom through a door, where basins stood on wooden plinths in rows and where there were baths and spotless tiled floors.

Well. If you'd walked me into the Ritz itself I couldn't have been more charmed. I'd never slept by myself, except for in hospital. I could clearly see that I would here. No more little legs and arms waking me in the night. No more pools of warm pee soaking into my skin when one of the others wet the bed, and no more complaints and cries out if I did. No more coats for warmth, no more bare mattress or springs in my back. This was the real deal.

The windows brought great light into that dormitory. It was a warm room and sterile in a way that reminded me of my beloved hospital. Miss Emily placed my suitcase on a bed half-way down the room and said, 'Put your stuff away, Frances. I will be back for you in a minute.'

She left and I opened my suitcase. It took me a minute to undo the knots of twine holding it closed. Inside were my few pieces of clothing that Sister Cecilia had given me and the nightie from hospital, which still fit because, to be honest, I didn't grow much as a child. I rummaged around in case my pencil case was in there, but no luck. I really wanted that back.

I didn't know either where they'd put my books, the ones Sister Cecilia had given me, and I fizzed inside with frustration. These nuns were taking everything and not listening to me at all. They were stealing my things. They took my pencil case, my pencils and my books and copies too.

Miss Emily returned with a bundle in her arms and placed it on the bed.

'Frances, you need to go wash yourself inside in the bathroom,' she said. She pointed at the door where she had shown me the bathroom, 'and use this soap.' She handed me a paper packet, 'then come back and get dressed into these,' she laid her hand on the bundle, 'and I will come for you in a short while, so don't dawdle.'

Looking back now as I tell this story, I know I was never destined for St Aidan's, the school beside the convent. From the moment I landed in that place I was there to work. They had a uniform ready for me, in a small size. That was the first place they took me when I arrived. I was a penitent in the eyes of those nuns the moment the parish priest got on the phone to them. They heard that a child was being molested and raped by her stepfather and they saw that child as a sinner who should be put to work. I was a fallen woman in their eyes, promiscuous and the cause of trouble for men. Nothing else explains any of it.

I didn't know it yet, but I wasn't there to get an education. I was there to serve time.

My crime?

It can only be that I told on Marty Murphy.

***

I finally got to the toilet, after my long journey and tour of the premises, and my bladder was relieved, although until that point it had forgotten itself in all the rigmarole. Then I washed myself, under my arms and my legs, my neck and face and hands. The soap felt nice. It was soft against my skin. I dressed in the uniform and brushed my hair. There were no mirrors, but I presumed I looked okay from the nod Miss Emily gave when she saw me.

Suddenly I was starving, so much so I thought I might vomit. Water filled my mouth and my tummy groaned. Miss Emily began to walk me through St Aidan's school again and we passed some sort of canteen, where I saw children sitting eating together at big tables. The smell of food hit me and I thought I would pass out. Surely I should be in there eating, I thought. It was past time for dinner.

But Miss Emily took me back through the musty tunnel instead. You can see that tunnel on old ordnance survey maps of the convent as a long thin building running from St Aidan's to the convent. The first part from the school had windows, but the last section that I think went under the church was underground and had no light at all except from the electric ones on the roof.

That tunnel was what separated me from the other kids. The tunnel brought me away from education, away from what I was promised, to the laundry where I did not belong.

This first day – thank God –when Emily brought me back through, I could smell food on that side as well and she delivered me into a large canteen instead of the laundry, where the women I had seen there now sat at round tables. At the top of the room the nuns sat in a row, at a table. I was pushed to sit at the only available seat. We were at full capacity it seemed. There was a knife, fork and spoon in front of me, and a cup. Thank God I was going to eat.

On our way there we passed a woman on her knees in the corridor with two nuns standing beside her. She was kneeling looking at the wall and I couldn't figure out what she was doing. I wondered if she was praying. There seemed to be a bowl of food spilled and a tray a little away, like it had been dropped. As I passed her a nun pushed her down to eat the food from the floor, like a dog. I had never seen anything like that before. It frightened me. The woman was crying and trying to eat it, but she kept falling forward so it was in her hair and eyebrows.

The nuns who pushed her down were saying, 'Eat that now. Eat that.'

I have heard other stories of that same punishment from other convents. The nuns must have swapped tips and tricks, it would seem.

22

NEW ROSS

Unlike the children's canteen, which was loud with the chatter of kids, the laundry canteen was deathly quiet but for the quiet scrape of forks and knives and the chewing of the women. It was strange and unusual.

It was tea time, well past dinner, and I had skipped a meal, so I was ravenous. I was given bread and dripping. Dripping is the fat left over after cooking meat, and in the convent it was left to go cool until it was like a soft paste and served with bread. I hated the smell of it and the texture, but I ate it in two bites. A nun sent me down another piece of bread with Miss Emily. I was also given a cup of watered-down milk.

I devoured both.

***

Recreation was a word I misunderstood for years. It actually means time spent at leisure, time spent on amusement or for a hobby. I thought it was another word for work, because in the Magdalene laundries, after we were fed every evening, we would all walk up in single file to begin our second jobs, which the nuns called 'recreation'. It was a factory.

That first night I followed the women from the dining room to this new recreation room. We passed the office I'd been in and the door was open. I scanned the room as I passed for my pencil case.

Our shuffle ended in a large square room with wooden chairs around a table, set almost like it was for dinner, but instead of plates there were biscuit tins, the kinds you get at Christmas.

I jumped to conclusions. Those were the tins Marty's aunts brought out when we visited. I thought this was going to be where we had tea and chatted and filled our faces with biscuits from those tins. I thought we might eat them and play games and sing like we sometimes did in school. Chairs aren't put around a table like that for no reason. Those biscuit tins were full, I was sure of it. This might be a party.

We all filed in and sat around the table and the women started opening the tins. The plump nun called me, 'Frances, sit here,' and she directed me to sit between two women at the top of the table. The nun sat over in the corner. I really wasn't into this name change. I was going to tell them I wanted to go home like Sister Cecilia said I could. I'd do it after this party.

I was handed a tin.

'Can I open it?' I said and was poked roughly by the nun sitting behind me.

'Pay attention,' she said, 'Teresa will tell you what you are to do.'

This must be a game, I realised.

Teresa opened my tin for me. There was not one biscuit inside, just plain-looking glass beads, all one colour and some silver ones and some silver crosses and medals. There was a roll of wire and some little things I didn't know the use of.

'So,' Teresa said, lifting out one or two beads and a hooked thing, 'you take this little bit here like this ...' she showed me, 'and loop that around there, through the hole, pull it back ... and do five, twist and another five,' she said, twisting and popping the beads on. It probably only took her twenty minutes to make the entire Rosary, twisting the wire through each bead and making little hooks onto which she added another bead. It looked so easy.

Then she handed it to me. 'Don't make a mistake,' she said, 'make sure to count them all the way around like this, one by one, ten, loop loop loop, and again, ten ... and then at the end it's this one,' the medal, 'and ten again and then this one,' the cross.

She held them up. A finished set of Rosary beads.

I did not get the hang of it quickly. It was not as easy as my instructor had made it look. Rosary beads are still an object I hate with a passion: the wire, the finicky string, the beads, one two three four five six seven eight nine ten ... is that ten? Did I miss one? One two three ...

My tin was full of the makings of endless orders of Rosary beads that the nuns had from the various church shops around the world, and from Rome itself. It was a factory for profit. I personally manufactured around a thousand Rosaries a year for Church coffers. Unpaid.

In fact, everything the women did there in New Ross was for profit and unpaid. We all worked ourselves to the bone and the nuns made a fortune. There we were in that little factory room, night in, night out, with the nuns pretending it was our leisure time, our hobby. All over the world, Catholics said their Rosaries every night with their fingers holding beads that slaves had strung together; some of them still do. It's absolutely disgraceful.

I was taught to knit in New Ross. I had learned before then of course. Most Irish children knew how to knit basic lines from around four or five, but in New Ross I learned how to knit properly, to follow intricate patterns, like herringbone and blackberry. The Aran jumpers we knitted at New Ross were cream sheep's wool with brown buttons, and they were sent off to be sold in America. The wool was greasy and dried out your hands, and the needles were too large for my small child's hands, but I was not given any concession on that part. I was in trouble all the time. And as a result, once I left there, I never knit another thing ever again.

If you made a mistake in the knitting, everyone suffered, because we were on a quota system – we had to have a certain amount done for the orders. So when I messed it up, and at twelve and thirteen I often did, the piece would be roughly grabbed from me by one of the other women and ripped out with frustration. You'd hear them start to tut as soon as your needles slowed down with the realisation that you'd missed a stitch and wasted so much time. That was the best option; having your knitting torn from your hands by an angry Maggie was better than one of the nuns seeing your mistake first. It wouldn't be your knitting torn, it would be your hair.

'You keep making the same mistake, Frances,' one of them might say. 'Will you ever learn it?'

At the time those things just made me more defensive. I felt angry. But I understand it now. Having a child in the group made their work harder.

We filled orders non-stop. Stickers on the filled boxes said Rome and Lourdes and all of those places where holiness is next to godliness. If there is a God, believe me, *she* isn't into slavery and the incarceration of women for nothing. Lost souls and broken hearts made those Rosaries that are, after all, made to chant words about an unmarried pregnant girl shunned by her community. *Blessed is the fruit of thy womb.* That is an irony that doesn't escape me.

The Church did such a number on Mary Magdalene too, made her into a prostitute when she was no such thing. They did to her what they did to all women – made us sinners or saints. They trapped Mary Magdalene, and they trapped me.

That first night I was so exhausted and incapable, I think I struggled to make one Rosary, and it was done wrong and ripped out by the nun. I was heavy-headed and my eyes were so sandy I couldn't focus at all. I was zoning out and falling asleep at my station. Don't forget I had come down that morning from Carlow and been on my feet since. One of the nuns poked me and then another one pulled me by the arm out of the room. She pulled me in silence through the laundry, down the convent and under the church, through the tunnel and up into St Aidan's, where the lights were off and the children were asleep. I was so relieved to see the bed.

I liked the sight of the children so much. I'd probably go with them all to school in the morning, I thought. Maybe I didn't go straight away because they didn't have things ready. Maybe they had to bring a chair or desk in. I let my imagination run on that, thought about myself in the morning sitting in class with my lovely pencil case while everyone looked at it with envy. I would be as proud as Punch.

'Sshhh,' said the nun who was dragging me, even though I wasn't speaking or making any noise I could stop. She was the one walking too fast, pulling me along so my feet hit the lino with a slap. I couldn't help that.

I saw the empty bed that I had been assigned.

'Go to bed,' she said.

I didn't need to be told twice. I stripped off into my nightie that was on top of my suitcase and climbed in. The feeling of the cold sheets against my tired legs and freshly bruised skin was soothing. My sore bones were cradled by this good mattress. I lay still, flooded by the relief of comfort. I held the sheet at my chest, lying on my back for a while as sleep pressed against my head. Then I turned over onto my tummy, a luxury I never had in a bed at home. It was a lovely feeling. I heard myself snore and jolted awake, grabbing onto the bed with fright. And, as I did, I remembered my Indian doll in my old school satchel that was in Sister Cecilia's office and I almost cried out. What would happen to it? I was momentarily panicked. Then heavier, darker shadows of sleep took over my conscious thought and I was gone.

***

When I say I was dragged out of that sleep, that is exactly what I mean. Dragged out of the bed by the arm, waking on the way and barely getting my feet under me so as not to drop to the floor. A nun stood there in the dark, a terrifying shadow. Out

137

the window, through the gap in the curtains, I could see the first peeks of sunlight on the horizon.

'Wake yourself,' the nun said in a hiss, and then pressed a finger to her lips. All the other children were still asleep. What time was this? I didn't even think I could hear a bird outside. It was so early.

She put her hand onto the bed as I got out of it. It was wet.

'You'll air that out later,' the nun said and then she pulled me across to the bathroom and told me to wash and dress. I was in that state of unfinished sleep that makes your head feel like it's stuffed with cotton wool, and though I splashed cold water on the back of my neck and face, I just could not wake up. The nun hissed at me over and over to hurry up as I tried to wash and dress, and I barely had my second shoe on when she grabbed me by the wrist and we started what was to be a routine march through the tunnel and over to the laundry.

We passed the empty classrooms and I was heartbroken.

The corridors in the convent were spotless and for good reason – they were cleaned most days. Most of the floors were tile and a few – the stairs and landings mostly – were the more modern vinyl. There were red corridors and ones with black and marble inlays. They were all scrubbed and polished until they were like mirrors.

By me.

***

The hallways of the laundry side of the convent, the extension side, were long and had lower ceilings than in the convent itself. In there, it felt like a church all over, with tall stained-glass windows and statues of the saints on every corner and bend. On the walls, I think, there were paintings of the nuns, or maybe not, perhaps it was saints and other things. The lighting was bad on the convent side, and in the winter we would struggle to check that the floors were polished with no streaks, given that there was barely any sunlight to see by in places. It was freezing cold on that side, with no heaters. Coming from those corridors into the baking hot laundry often made me queasy and faint.

The first morning, when I was trotted down through the tunnel into the convent, I saw ahead of me women on their knees scrubbing the tiled floors of the laundry wing. There was a pair of women at one end, with another woman behind them, and they were on their knees working into the middle, scrubbing the marks away. There were teams it seemed on each end. One team was missing a scrubber. It had only one, and the lady behind. I had a sinking feeling I was about to become involved in this.

I was right. The nun barked at me to get to work as if I was a trained-up, fully-in-the-know adult and not a twelve-year-old, confused child. She pointed at my scrubbing partner, a middle-aged woman looking up at me with huge brown eyes, a long chin and a nose that gave her a hang-dog expression, only added to by her hair, parted in the middle and forming cocker spaniel ears that fell to each side. She was sitting on her heels waiting for me to start scrubbing from this side; there were two silver buckets and a basin waiting there for me too.

In the basins there was hot water and wooden scrubbing brushes floating in it. I went down to sit on my heels too, after a push from the nun, and the other lady lifted the brushes and handed one to me. It was roasting hot and I let it drop.

My head spun from an instant slap. The nun hissed, 'Don't do that again.'

My scrubbing partner looked at me with a sad smile, and showed me how to soap up the brush, rubbing it fast so it made a *thwack-thwack* sound, and then she bent forward and soaped up the full square of the tile ahead of her.

'Square by square, girl,' she said. Her accent was like mine.

I had never scrubbed a floor. Our cottage was made of mud and sawdust, and in Roncalli Place my mother did the floors after we had left for school to save any footprints. I followed the woman next to me, did what she did. Taking the marks off the floor was satisfying at first, but soon it started to burn my arms and back, and my knees were scorched from dragging my skin as I moved forward. Every square we scrubbed the little woman behind us dried the tile we had left. I was so small my whole body fit into the perimeter of the tile I was scrubbing.

Halfway to the middle I began to get really upset. I can't remember what started me off, probably thinking about my Indian doll or my pencil case, but I could feel the sting of tears behind my eyes.

I wanted my granny.

I whispered to the women, 'Excuse me,' but they didn't answer or look up. I stopped and put my hand in the air like you might if you had a question. I suppose I did have a question. I had a hundred of them. Where is the classroom? Why am I here? Where is this place? Why am I scrubbing floors when Sister Cecilia said I was going to a new school and getting a wonderful education?

Where was my pencil case?

I raised my hand higher. 'Excuse me.'

The little old woman behind me flicked me with her drying rag.

'Sshhh,' she said, 'get on with it.' I looked behind at her and she shook her head, pinching her eyes shut in a clear expression of *stop it*. She pressed a finger to her lips. The nail was missing on it.

My tears fell onto the tiles and I scrubbed them away. There was a growing sense of panic in me. Like young animals do when they are afraid, I wanted my mother. I wanted to go home.

I said to the lady right next to me, 'Excuse me, where is the class?'

She looked at me as though I was crazy and told me to get on with it too.

I looked back again at the old lady.

'Just shut up,' she hissed and looked down.

Surely they knew I was in the wrong place? Why weren't they telling me I should be in school, like most adults always did if you were dawdling and late, or when you were kept home sick but Mammy sent you just down to the shop because fresh air would do you good? Adults were always poking their noses in, always asking questions, why were these ones not?

I looked at my hands all of a sudden to check I was still me. It struck me that maybe I was somehow a grown-up now, or had jumped into a different body, like the sci-fi stories I heard from Paddy. But no, I was still me. Those were my hands. I knew from my freckles.

Why were these women being so strange? Why were they not talking?

I was Alice down a rabbit hole, in a world that wasn't behaving itself, where everything was back to front and upside down.

Where adults were treated like children and where children, where I, was being asked to behave like an adult. It was torture. Sister Cecilia told me I was going to a new school, and now here I was on some sort of weird chain gang.

What was going on?

I was shown, then, how to tie small squares of blanket that Miss Emily called 'shiners' to my feet with string, and we would scuff the squares with them, to polish them till they were gleaming. Up and down, shuffle shuffle, up and down.

I came to know that routine well. Up at dawn, sweep, scrub, eat, pray at Mass, laundry, eat, laundry, eat, make Rosaries, sleep, repeat.

I still hear the nuns clapping hands in my sleep sometimes, the often welcome and simultaneously dreaded signal that we were to move on to our next task.

23

THE CALENDAR

We scrubbed the floors and met in the middle and that was that job done. I rubbed my knees as I followed the other women back around to where the convent door was open, expecting us to join the others – who had been scrubbing elsewhere – for breakfast. One of the women clucked her tongue at me in a soft way when we went in, like you might to a pup, and it felt kind. She shooed me into my place with a gentle hand. I wanted more of that.

I sat on my seat at the round table at the back of the room and someone placed a bowl of watery porridge in front of me. I was so hungry I spooned half of it into me so fast I gasped and nearly threw it back up.

'Frances, eat slowly,' a passing nun called out. I took a breath and chewed the next spoon of slop carefully.

Nobody was talking. My thoughts were childish, most about the size of people's noses, or their hairy chins. I wished Paddy was there so I could whisper to him and giggle. Then I thought about my pencil case again and felt so bad about it. I had no sophistication in how I thought – of course I didn't – so it made things worse. I couldn't grasp that my pencil case was gone, or that I wasn't going to school, or what this place was at all. I remember wondering if the women were deaf, because nobody spoke back to me, but then I knew they couldn't be because they always told me to shush. I wondered were they a type of nun, even though I could see their hair and legs. They weren't novices, I knew that, because they didn't have white dresses and red lips like the ones I'd seen in drawings and movies.

It was baffling. But what was worse was that nobody sat me down and said, 'You live here now. You'll work every day. You're not going to school. It's over,' so I didn't know. It was a torture of the mind that was inflicted on every inmate in that so-called asylum, that workhouse. But I suppose grown women would have worked it out pretty quickly or been advised of it from the get-go. I was a little kid. The word penitent was meaningless to me, though I had heard it before in Mass when the collections would go around. I did not know that women in Ireland were being sent to prison for stepping over the line set down by their local priest, whatever he decided it was. Maybe he thought they were promiscuous, maybe he thought they were too outspoken or not submissive enough, because the women in New Ross were not pregnant women, not when I arrived anyway. Whatever we had all done – at least to get there – had nothing to do with illegitimate babies.

As I scraped my bowl with the spoon for the last lick, a nun passed by me again and I turned quickly in my chair and caught her eye and said, 'Am I going to school today? When am I going to school?'

She ignored me completely and walked by. I watched her all the way to the top of the line, thinking maybe she would ask the nuns sitting up there and come back to me with an answer, but she didn't. She just turned left and walked around again. She mustn't have heard me, I thought, so when she came around again, I said it louder, 'Am I going to school now?' But she just walked by again.

So I turned back around and asked the lady sitting straight across from me the same question. She stared at me, hard-eyed. I asked again.

'Am I going to go to school today?'

She shook her head and pressed her finger really hard on her lips.

As we left the dining hall in single file, I asked the woman behind me, and then I asked the woman in front of me. I asked the nun who walked us all down to Mass, and then I asked the nun who walked us all back to the laundry. I asked everyone all day long, 'When is school? When am I going to school?'

Not one person answered me. The nuns acted like they didn't hear me as they jogged me back and forth along the corridors so roughly my voice bounced in my throat. But I asked anyway, because I needed to let out the building desperation that was pressure inside of me. Sister Cecilia had told me I was going to a new school. And there was a school here so why was I not in it? I wanted to be there, with the other children, learning from books that I loved. Someone had to tell me the answer to that. So I kept on asking.

And asking.

And asking.

And asking.

They just ignored me.

***

We were brought to Mass, one nun at the top of the line of Magdalene women, one at the end, and one walking along the side. You see that same formation when prisoners are moved from one place to another. We were missing the shackles, but that was the only difference.

In the church, which was attached to the convent in an L-shape, we were seated beside the nuns. From where I was, I could see the children from the school file in together holding hands and sitting in rows along the side, but nobody could see me – the Magdalenes were kept around the corner out of sight. Outsiders came in from the locality, a handful of them, and there were teachers and workers too. The nuns sat all along the sides and a priest stood at the altar, facing the nuns and us. But the outsiders couldn't see any of us at all.

When the hymns began I was glad to sing, and the women around me were singing too. It was restful and my body relaxed with the long exhales of notes of the songs I knew. From where I sat, I could see intricate patterns on the ceiling, a design of roses and sharp edges, and pillars that stretched up to the tallest part. Stations of the cross ran around the back of me and, as the priest droned on in Latin, I looked at them. Jesus with brambles tight against his head, blood running in rivers down his face. I knew the pain of brambles, the way the thorns dug in when you were fighting against your brothers' hands for blackberries down the way from Granny's cottage. We used to collect blackberries in tins and bring them back and Granny would stew them up with sugar into a hot jam, mashing them with a fork over the heat of the fire. One of our drinking jars would be filled with it and that would do us for weeks. She would spread it onto bread and bring it out with us.

I thought about Duckett's Grove and the river. If I could go back now I would even swim, I swore to that bleeding man in the painting. I begged him with my mind to let me go back. And for a moment I thought I felt the air change and I was by the river with Granny. I could hear the soft murmur of the weir just up the way. I could feel the softest papery hand on the back of my neck as Granny pulled my curls away to fix the collar of my coat.

I was thumped awake back into the convent church. Thumped back into the real world. I looked up and the plump nun was staring down at me with a face like thunder. She flashed her eyes and I focused myself on looking intent on whatever prayer was going right then.

Etnenosind ... asintentat ... sedliberanos ... lo ... Amen.

***

After Mass I was brought past the laundry into the yard. There was a man standing there, a stout older man scratching his head and fiddling with a tape measure, and when I was brought out he huffed and puffed and waddled over. He had a cigarette in his mouth, burned almost down to the end, a pencil behind his ear and his overalls were filthy and covered in paint. He stretched the tape all the way from my feet to my head and took his pencil down, saying something about 'too small', and wrote numbers on a filthy piece of paper he had taken out of his pocket. Then he started fussing again and had me stand against the wall instead, marking a line where my head was and two more lines along the wall against the sides of my feet. After that he beckoned me away and measured all of those and wrote those down. He went back inside, so did I, and he started measuring the calendar machine I had been shown the day before. He was humming and hawing and grumbling, and I stood there watching him. I wanted to ask him if I was going to school, but it didn't seem right to and he never looked me in the eyes.

Before he was finished, the nun told me to get back to turning the handle of the mangle again, and I did, or at least I tried to. I had to stretch up and over to reach the handle, and stand on my toes to pull it down, and it would fly back with momentum and pull me off my feet at first when it went back up.

I got the hang of how to stay on the ground while turning that mangle handle, but before long my armpits were paining me with the constant stretching action it took to avoid it. The mangle was called the wringer sometimes in New Ross, depending on who was calling it. The jolt it gave me as it came around hurt my neck. I was a small child for my age. Neglect and malnutrition had me in clothes for eight-year-olds – I remember the tags on the items Sister Cecilia picked out for me from the pile. I had had the same coat for years.

Once my box was made, they moved me onto the larger calendar machine and I stayed there working on that machine the whole time I was at New Ross. Whereas a mangle was used to get water out of clothes, the calendar was used to get the washing creases out of wet sheets. It was, I suppose, a huge iron. The big barrel that rolled around and around was heated with electricity, and it was roasting hot. Hot as any iron would be. The sheets would be fed in one side, creased, but as flat as they could be made by the women, folded end to end to get two sides done at once. And in it would go and come out ironed and dried so the women could fold it. Sometimes, if I went too slow, the sheet would get marked and you'd get in terrible trouble for that, or if I went too fast it wouldn't be dried properly and there'd be a whack or a poke in the back with a crucifix to tell you to speed up. So I knew from that first day to get the rhythm right. But it was a hard, hard job.

The nuns oversaw all the work. The plump one, the 'watcher' I called her, she sat on a high stool at the back of the room, fiddling with her Rosary beads and watching with hawk eyes for anything that was wrong. It was her crucifix you'd feel in your back, always. She would ram it into your ribs without a word, like a cattle prod, and it always left a bruise. You couldn't make a mistake – it wasn't worth it.

My despair after twenty-four hours in the laundry was forming in my throat as a lump I couldn't swallow and tears I couldn't cry. I thought my throat was going to close over and it crossed my mind I might not be able to eat. But by the time the bell went for dinner I was so hungry from work I forgot all about everything else but food.

***

I do ask myself now what those nuns were doing, selling women out like that? It's so easy to dismiss them as a group – the nuns – as if they were a school of fish. But these were Irish women, like me, like my mother. Women who had grown up with their own mothers and sisters and school friends in this country, women who knew first-hand how hard women had it here. There isn't any way that, out of all of those nuns there, not one of them had suffered as a child like I did, or close to it. There's no way at least one of them didn't have a childhood like mine. Because the truth of that is it was common. So how could they stand there watching me and all these other women work like that, the way they did? How could they treat us with more contempt than a prison warden has for murderers? How could they stand there throwing stones at us, when we weren't the sinners?

How could they be so cruel and so horrible, when surely they knew that there but for the grace of God went every single one of them?

Day in, day out those nuns, those women and others like them, watched me at twelve, thirteen, fourteen and on until I was nearly an adult, work to the bone. They watched me, but not only that, they made it as hard for me as they could. They made me do hard time, hard penance, for a crime a man had committed against me. Something I had no control over. If I had taken a knife and gutted Marty Murphy like I had often dreamed about, at least prison would have let me go to school. But not in New Ross. I was given nothing – no books, pens or paper. I wasn't allowed to speak. Can you think of it? I spent my entire teenage years without so much as a conversation. Those days when we are supposed to moon over film stars and pop stars and walk to school begrudgingly because you'd rather be listening to music and dreaming about boys ...? Mine were spent in a hot, sweaty laundry house, seven days a week, pulling sheets filled with scalding water and feeding them through a hot iron. Pushing that handle up and over until I was doing it in my sleep, avoiding the eyes of the other broken hearts in that room so I wouldn't so much as smile at them, to avoid the dig of the end of a crucifix into my ribs if I was caught.

If I think back then, the earliest you were formally allowed to leave school was fifteen. I could be wrong, but I think most did and I would have left too around then I'm sure. I would have left school at fifteen and gone into the factories with my friends on the back of the primary certificate we got at thirteen or fourteen. But I went into the laundry just at the beginning of fifth class, and so I never got any certificates at all. There is no justification for what the nuns did. I don't believe Sister Cecilia was lying to me. I think she thought she was sending me to St Aidan's and that someone told her I would go there. I believe she felt sorry for me, wanted to help and change things and thought it was the right thing to do. She could see I was bright, and I know I was, and she wanted to help me learn so I could make something of myself. She wouldn't have known about the treatment kids got there; all of that didn't come out until years after. She thought it was a school she was sending me to, not a chain gang.

The nuns took what she promised away from me. They stole my pencil case, they stole my education, they stole my formative years, they stole my young experiences with love and friends and life.

When the girls my age in Carlow were leaving school and going into factories and behind shop counters, I was incarcerated. When Irish girls were screaming and pulling their hair out over the Beatles in Dublin when they played there, I was making Rosary beads in a room of old women.

While all of you were growing up, I was closing up and closing in.

My teens are a blur of laundry and beads, that's the extent of it.

151

Marty took everything from me, but what was the point of locking me up instead of him? It wasn't like he was the one keeping my mother and her children fed anyway – she was the one with two jobs. Why was I punished for his wrong? Then I think about it and I realise that's always the way, women are always the ones to blame when men act badly. It's what we were wearing, what we said, what we did. Deep down the Church must have seen me as some sort of Jezebel, at ten or eleven years of age, as innocent as you like; some sort of Eve leading man to sin.

Even if they didn't. Even if they were keeping me there to save me from him, if it was the only way, why were they so cruel to me? Why were they so hard? I was a little kid, yet they never let me have a minute to look at a book or sing a song. I had no ropes to jump with or wheels to push, or even a doll to keep me company. I didn't get to run around or dance. I was made into a miniature robot for the Church to profit from.

That was so wrong, what they did to me.

In New Ross I would lie in bed at night wondering when I would get back to Carlow. I'd always rejected other kids, always told them to leave me alone, but now I wanted to see them. I wanted them to crowd around me trying to look at my Indian doll. If I could go back, I'd even let them play with her if they asked me. I just wanted to be back in my own school, not here. I swore if I could just go back I wouldn't say no to the games – I wanted to play hopscotch on hot footpaths, and throw the stone from chalked squares. I wanted to run in to huge swinging ropes and chant familiar rhymes as I jumped over and under in time.

I thought about those things, and focused on that loss because I could not think of Granny. I refused to allow her face to appear in my thoughts, because when she did the longing for her arms would be so strong it would stop my breath. I missed her so much I had to shut off from that part of what I knew was back in Carlow. But sometimes, if I let my guard down when I got into bed at night, her lovely gentle face would cross my mind and I would get a hard lump in my throat and tears would roll down my nose onto the pillow. Once or twice I deliberately let my mind float up and out the window and back to Bennekerry. I would pretend the mattress I was lying on was my granny's body, and I would shut my eyes so tight I could almost feel the rise and fall of her chest as I fell asleep.

24

THE TUNNEL

I was dragged through the tunnel twice a day – first thing in the morning before the other children woke and last thing at night when they were still asleep. That was the routine from day one. The tunnel was terrifying and I dreaded that part of the journey; it was dark, black in corners with dim fluorescent lights that hummed and flickered. It was a horror movie down there and being pulled through it by a silent nun scared me deeply.

There were rooms off it, I think, barely lit beyond their open doors and looking back now I realise they must have been storage rooms, but as a child I worried they were tombs and the boxes in them, coffins. My eyes saw things that weren't there every time we went through. I saw spiders, rats and ghosts. I flinched at sounds and at imagined movements in the dark. I was scared.

I went through a lot in New Ross – I was hit, smacked, poked, kicked and humiliated – but the worst thing I went through was being locked down in that tunnel in the dark and they did that to me a lot.

I was called away from my station sometimes, usually by the fat watcher – 'Frances!' – and I'd look up and see another nun there. 'Go with Mother now,' she would say.

Go with? I was dragged away, yanked along by the cardigan. The first time it happened, this routine, I thought perhaps I was going to school after all, as we headed for the tunnel. But when she opened the door, instead of walking through it dragging me with her, she just pushed me in.

'Stay in here,' she said, and then she switched off the light and closed the door behind her.

I cried out, 'No!' but I heard a chink of the keys in the lock as she locked me in.

Chills ran across my shoulders and I banged on the door, 'Don't lock it,' I said. But I heard her footsteps leave.

I could see nothing. I felt every spider of my imagination creep out of the holes in the wet walls. My eyes adjusted slightly, but that was worse. Every corner held a monster, every shadow was a clawing, creeping creature out for my blood. The quiet was replaced with shuffling feet, the clank of chains. I heard skirts, and moans, and animal sounds. I was petrified. I remembered the banshee from Granny's stories and became convinced she was behind me, so I spun around with a shriek, but there was nothing there. So I huddled on my hunkers where I had been left, blind in the dark. I checked over my shoulder again and again. My hands flew up to slap at imaginary insects on my shoulders and arms and neck.

I tried to pretend this was the tunnel in Duckett's Grove, and that Granny was there too, and Paddy and Michael. I hummed to myself the little songs that Granny always sang. For a moment I managed it. I was there not here. But it faded away.

My legs went dead, so I stood up again until they recovered, and the pins and needles that came after that had me in tears.

I have no idea how long I was left there the first time, but hiding me in the pitch-black tunnel became a routine. The other inmates told me that I was being hidden because the 'men with the suits' had arrived in the laundry. I connected those events and started to dread cars pulling into the yard in case it would happen again. And it always did.

I lived on edge. The sudden appearance of a nun at the door of the laundry and I would be thrown down there for God knows how long. I was so, so afraid of it.

Those men in suits were likely the state inspectors. They were sent around to all of the Magdalene laundries in Ireland to check on conditions. They must have been blind to clear any of them. In New Ross all of the women were in very poor health, overworked and undernourished. When I remember their faces, I see the gaunt expression of people in a workhouse. Bones and sunken eyes. Yet along came these men in suits, who nodded and probably had a cup of tea and some cake with the nuns, and signed us away again and again.

On one occasion I was put into the tunnel and forgotten about. When the men in suits left, nobody came to get me. The nuns didn't notice and the day in the laundry continued. If the women noticed they didn't say anything or weren't listened to. I was in there for hours. I know I went in before the first Angelus bell because I heard it ringing when I was down there. I also heard the second. When they finally came to get me, they just brought me straight up to bed and all the other children were asleep.

Being down there in the dark for so long had an irreversible effect on me and I am still afraid of the dark now. I was convinced ghosts were with me. I could hear them chatter. I thought they were women who had been sent down there too. I was afraid their fingers would reach around the doors of those tombs and grab me in. My body shook from real terror.

I often had to wee down there. The first time I held it for so long I was in pain with it and eventually had to squat down, pull down my pants and pee onto the floor. I cried the whole time in loud sobs, so sure I was that I would be swung for it. When they eventually remembered me, at the very end of the day, and came and switched on the light, they saw the pools of pee. But they said nothing about it at all, they just dragged me along and up to the dormitory.

I dream, sometimes, that I am in the tunnel again and the ghosts come out of the rooms and claw me.

**

Bedtime for the workers in New Ross was late, but I have no idea what time it actually was that we would be sent off from our Rosary-making. I would be dragged through the tunnel by the arm, thrown up the stairs and into the bed in the middle of a whole dormitory full of sleeping children. The nuns moved silently but viciously.

Sometimes I would see a pair of open eyes watching me as I was dragged across the floor and pushed into the empty bed. A mystery child.

I was never allowed go to bed without an escort. I was never let sleep past the other children's bell. I was last in, first out.

A ghost.

I used to lie in that bed every night, exhausted but awake, and I would stare for a moment before I shut my eyes at the head in the next bed and wonder about that child. I fixated on her as my lost friend, the one I would have if they let me go to school. Her skin was so white it almost glowed in the dark, framed with those sticky curls that children get when they're out for the count. The way their eyes sink a little and their cheeks get rosy. That's what the nuns would have seen too in my bed when they came in to drag me out of it. I wonder did they ever want to leave me sleeping?

When I was being pulled down to the laundry to start scrubbing every single day before dawn, I always looked at the other kids still sleeping, where I knew I was supposed to be too. That's how I felt.

Sometimes, as the nun would be standing there impatiently waiting for me to pull on my smock and cardigan, I'd imagine that I could see my brother Paddy's face come round the door, and he would call me to run away and I would. Sometimes it felt so real ... I'd be roughly dragged back down through that dark tunnel and I'd pretend it was a game, and we were in Duckett's Grove and this was that tunnel. There was no nun, no laundry, it was all make-believe with Granny. But it never was.

I would have made a deal by the end of the first week to go back to live with Marty, I missed Carlow and my family so much. I swear I must have asked the nuns every hour of every day for the first six months: 'When am I going to school?' My childish head wouldn't give up on it. They never answered me.

Why didn't they? They should have said 'never' on day one and been done with it. But they broke me down this way. I spent the whole first year at the Magdalene laundry baffled, frustrated and upset.

Perhaps the Good Shepherds did save me ... someways. Pain from home was replaced with a different set of pains: burns and scalds, the jab of a crucifix in the ribs, or a pinch. But also an unsettling soreness that only those of us who have been imprisoned understand. It's not a sore throat or a headache, but a vague sense of both maybe. The sense that I'd never get back out into the world, that I'd never do nothing again.

Back in Carlow, doing nothing was a comfort to me. I used to go and drape myself over this big metal gate that was the entrance to a field, one of those ones made of tubes of steel welded together, so it had no sharp edges. I'd climb up onto the bottom bar and let my arms hang over the top – like an old coat left there. In that field you'd see lots of things. Fox cubs dancing around their mother, whimpering as she barked at them to leave her alone, trying to wean them. Their little black noses and eyes were like buttons on a teddy. In the haze of the evenings I would watch them for hours. Tractors pulling the clods of earth up and to the side with big metal ploughs, forcing the hard ground soft again. The man would wave at me every time he came back to that end to turn. I never waved back, I just watched him. The way he slouched in the seat, one hand on the wheel, his white hips packed into his trousers where his shirt didn't reach. The way he pulled on his cigarette and blew it out, and the smell of it in the air. Potato pickers in short sleeves, following the spinner as it lifted potatoes out of the ground. The way they'd bend in a rhythm to save their backs, up and down. My granny always did that job to make some extra money, but she was last on the farmers' lists because she was old, so she always had to wait till last minute. There'd be squalling baby birds in the hedgerows, and I'd press my cheek to the metal tubes of the gate and listen to them scream for food. The mother bird would pass in and out of the breaks in branches with her mouthful of food for them. She would harass me if I went near them, I knew that from experience. As they got older, she would line them up along the metal of the gate and feed them there. They were cute, all fluffed up with their big mouths, and she never stopped going back and forth, filling their bellies to get them through the night. I wished I was a bird sometimes.

Sometimes, in the evenings, hundreds of starlings would crowd there to peck the tilled earth for worms and grubs. Then they'd ascend into the sky in unison, drawing shapes in the sky.

I escaped with them, for those moments. And when they left, they took some of my pain too and left me fresh.

In the convent I had no way to find that time, looking back now. So I think I was driven to a sort of insanity at first. The frustration built itself too high to contain and I had nowhere to let the pain go. I was constantly fatigued, stressed and close to madness. I couldn't let it go, why was I here? When was I going to school? Where was my pencil case?

They just ignored me.

Although the nuns would teach me and preach to me that suffering was good, it didn't feel good. I would stare at Christ on the cross and think he was a fool. He could have escaped. Why didn't he? Why didn't his father save him? Why couldn't mine?

I was held and hurt and trapped and nobody was coming

for me at all. I had nothing. They had taken the world from me when they'd taken my pencil case.

And I couldn't even find a moment to let it settle. I couldn't stare into space or watch out the window or I'd be slapped, poked or kicked back to work. So I forced the pain inward, and it bubbled and built until I absolutely lost it.

I had been dragged out of bed the morning before as always and sent in to wash my face and use the toilet before work. The nun always stood at the bathroom door when I did that, and on this day when I walked into the bathroom, I met another child. A small girl with brown curly hair was standing at the end of the room.

I may as well have seen a ghost.

'Hello,' she said, so I said hello back.

'Where do you go every day? You're not in the school with all of us.'

I didn't answer. I was not sure what to say.

Then the nun came in and grabbed me out, telling the child very sternly to get back to her bed.

When I went to bed that night, instead of being taken to my bed in St Aidan's, I was now squashed in beside the window in the sleeping quarters of the Magdalene women. I never went back to St Aidan's dorm. My fate was sealed. I was never going to school.

And that was playing over and over in my head that morning as I scrubbed the corridors with the other women, ruining my knees and burning my hands. And I remembered Sister Cecilia had said I could come back to Carlow if I wasn't happy in the new place. So as soon as the nun came to bring us to Mass I said, 'I've decided I want to go back to Carlow,' and I said it with a childish confidence, because I felt as though I had Sister Cecilia behind me.

She ignored me.

I said, 'Excuse me, excuse me, I want to go back to Carlow,' and she ignored me again.

I ran to keep up with her. One of the women tried to catch me as I passed her, to pull me back, seeing what I was doing was not going to end well, but she didn't manage to reach out in time and I caught up to the nun.

'Excuse me, excuse me,' I said, 'I want to go back now. I want to go to Carlow.'

She ignored me and so I reached out and took her sleeve and pulled it, and because I was small and running, it created a momentum that spun her around and knocked her a little. She stood on her own skirt and almost fell, and when she steadied herself, well, the anger within her was beyond anything you could imagine. The nuns were so unhappy, so understimulated and institutionalised themselves, violence erupted in them so easily.

And it did then. She got me by the hair and pushed me back into the wall, ramming her other arm up and into my neck. She bared her teeth and pulled and pushed until my face was turned sideways and I was totally pinned there.

'You'll observe silence,' she seethed.

'I want to go home to Carlow. Sister Cecilia said I could,' I said.

'I don't care what Sister whoever said to you,' the nun said, 'there is no talking here, you'll be quiet.'

Another nun, one of the older, fatter ones who I'd see rarely, usually only at Mass, appeared then. Her eyes flashed when she saw the scene in front of her.

I struggled against her. I kicked out. Why wouldn't they let me go to school? What was I even here for? I didn't want to do laundry.

'Let me go!' I screamed it, bucking against the hands that held me back. 'Let me ...!' I kicked out.

The second nun rounded in on me with a hard slap to the side of my face and another in quick succession to my shoulder. I wriggled and dropped my weight, slid out of the first nun's grasp and onto the floor. But they dropped too, got on top of me, and they started to slap me over and over. The more I howled, the harder the slaps got.

'Silence!' they said with each hard slap.

'I want to go to home, I want my pencil case.' I said it over and over, determined not to be broken, determined to make myself understood. I did not want to stay. Why were they making me stay? Sister Cecilia said I could come home.

They slapped me and slapped me and slapped me.

'You'll be silent!' I was told. 'You're not going back to Carlow. Nobody wants you in Carlow. Your mother dumped you here and not even she wants you.'

They were lying. I told them so. They slapped and slapped.

The other women watched them do it, watched as they stood me back up each time they thought they had me defeated and watched me tell them again, 'I want to go to Carlow. I want my pencil case.' They watched them slap me down again, instructing me to keep silent, pushing me onto my knees and forcing me to do penance for sins I hadn't committed. I kept getting to my feet and they'd slap and push me back. They wanted to break me.

I started to squeal, scream and roll back and forth, pushing away their slapping hands, climbing out of their grasps as they tried to restrain me. I had had enough of this. I rolled away and got to my feet. Then I picked up a plant pot that sat in the nook by the door of the corridor and threw it over my head onto the tiles, smashing it into smithereens in front of the shocked Magdalene women and the furious nuns.

When I went to bed that night, in the dorm with the other Magdalene women, one thought rolled over and over in my head. The answer that I had been looking for was set in the marks on my skin. I wasn't going to school. I wasn't going home. I was staying here.

***

Whenever I wet the bed in New Ross I would be treated as though I had done it out of laziness or vindictiveness. Even then it never made sense to me. Why on earth would they think I would rather lie in my own cold wee than take a few steps across the room to the bathroom? Now of course we know it can be a sign of stress in children, but we didn't then. When I was a child I wet the bed most nights.

In New Ross sometimes you'd get away with it. We made our own beds when we got up and so if the nun who woke me wasn't vigilant, or if it was the time of year when I would be woken in the dark, I'd cover it up and come back to it later. Much of the time the nun wouldn't notice. My nightdress would be put down to the laundry and washed and the bed was made and so I'd avoid the punishment. Then I would be so tired getting into bed at night and I could tuck the blanket under my back to try to avoid the damp patch. But when I was caught, and I often was, I would be fetched from the laundry that afternoon and told to bring the mattress downstairs to air it out, by walking around the yard between the convent and the school with the mattress on my back.

I hated doing that. It was humiliating, which I suppose was part and parcel of the punishment. The mattresses we slept on in New Ross were luxurious compared to the old things we had at home, but by today's standards they were thin. They were a thick pad of something soft, maybe foam or cotton, and covered in thick striped material and held together with large buttons. They weren't heavy like they are today, and the nun would help you drag it to the bottom of the stairs and lift it onto your back. The mattress would bend forward and press against your head as you walked around and around outside, sometimes with the company of another bedwetter walking around and around with you. If it was raining, you'd be told to lean the mattress up against the open window and stand beside it, on view as a bedwetter. The belief was the shame would get to you and you'd give up. But sure, what do sleeping children know about bedwetting until they wake up wet?

Once, later, when I was sleeping in the dorm with the Magdalene women instead of the children, I woke up again in a wet bed and I just could not face the repeat of every other time – the way you'd be asked why you did it and humiliated in the same way. So I took the wet sheet and blanket off my bed, and when everyone got up and was washing in the bathroom, I swapped them for the clean dry ones off the bed next to mine. It belonged to an older lady, I don't remember her name, but I remember her coming back to it to get her cardigan and she realised with a gasp what had been done to her.

She just turned and stared right at me and pulled her sheet and blankets all the way back off the mattress. Those were sopping yellow with wee, but her mattress was bone dry.

'Did you wet your bed?' the nun said, seeing what she was doing. 'I'm surprised at you,' she said.

'I did not, Mother,' the old lady said and she just stared straight at me.

'But the ...' the nun looked at the bed and then the mattress, and then followed the woman's gaze to where I stood.

'Did someone swap your bed out?' the nun said to the woman.

The woman said nothing. She just shook her head while looking at me and then she turned around and took the sheet and blanket off her bed, rolled it in a ball and said, 'I'll get these to the laundry,' with a pursed mouth.

I wasn't admitting anything, I stood my ground. I needed one day at least without walking around with that mattress on my back.

***

But Karma came to call, in a way. At least I thought it did.

They didn't offer water in the laundry. Nothing to quench the thirst that would build up no matter how much you tried to ignore it until you were driven mad.

You were given tea or milk to drink at meals and that was all you got, though you worked your back off in searing heat all day long. So we used to drink water from the sinks in the toilet. My worst day in the laundry came over that. It was in the early afternoon and I had been working all day non-stop, except for the short break for dinner. My mouth wouldn't let up. It was dry and sticky, and I couldn't swallow. The dinner had been salty ham and cabbage, and my body wasn't able for the salt. My mind was consumed with a need for water. But I waited it out. If I went too soon, I wouldn't be let go to the toilet again and I always needed to go after dinner. So I timed it right and went to the toilet. I ran the tap and scooped the water into my mouth with my cupped hands over and over until I felt okay again. I did that until my thirst was quenched. The cold water ran down my chin and onto my hot, sticky neck and I rubbed it around the back. I leaned on the sink bowl, rested my forehead against the tile. I don't know how long I was there. I pressed my recent burn against the cold and felt the relief.

Then I went into the toilet and sat down.

Suddenly I heard what can only be described as a snarl from outside the door and a voice. 'Frances!'

It was a nun, one I barely had dealings with day to day. The cold bathroom went from a small place of respite from the hell heat of the laundry to one of fury as the nun kicked the door, screaming my name. As soon as I opened it she caught me by the hair, on the side over my ear, and pulled me down, dragging me out along the floor and slamming me against the legs of the wash stand. I yelled.

'Were you smoking?' she said.

I was stunned. What?

'Smoking, I knew it! I knew it!!' she said and she began to batter me with her closed fists about the head as I crouched against the wall.

'I never did smoke,' I squealed through the gasps, 'Mother, I never-'

167

But she kept going, punching me until she lost the strength in her arms, and then she kicked me as I curled up on the floor covering my head as best I could while keeping an eye on her feet and hands. She was frothing at the mouth, spitting prayers as she did it. Her eyes were dark and almost closed as she looked at me through slits.

'I knew it! You filthy girl,' she said over and over, and prayed while she pulled me over and about, kicking as I tried to stop her. I pushed her hands, her feet, but it made her worse and soon I decided to give in – I went limp, a rag doll thrown around the bathroom like I was nothing.

When she finally wore out and stopped, she was purple in the face, her black wimple tight on her scrunched cheeks as she drew breaths in and let them out like a boxer in a ring.

'Filthy girl!' she said, gathering up one more bit of strength to drag me back to the laundry, bruises already forming on my cheeks and eyes, my lip swollen and bleeding, my ear throbbing.

'Get back to work!' she said, and nobody caught my eye at all as I did.

25

PENANCE

In the 1911 census, the women at the Magdalene asylum in New Ross are recorded as 'inmates'. But when I was there, they called us 'penitents'. It means a person who seeks forgiveness for their sins. There were no sinners in New Ross. Just victims, victims of the patriarchy, victims of misogyny.

There is a memorial to us in the school that is now in the laundry building there – I was shown it when I visited recently. The word 'penitents' is used on that, and it really stood out to me and I was very hurt by it. The women in New Ross laundry were not sinners, or bad ones; we were innocent women. That memorial and the wording of it showed me that people still think we deserved it, we asked for it, we brought it on ourselves. That word is loaded.

So many Irish people will still argue that the laundries were places of refuge for women who had 'gotten themselves into trouble'. What trouble? In our laundry there were no babies that I knew of, but even if there were, pregnancy is natural, babies aren't trouble. The Magdalene laundries weren't refuges. They were prisons, places of punishment. They were workhouses, chain gangs, slave labour camps. They made slaves of us. They sold us, and sold our babies. They abused us, hid us away. They let many of us die.

I've been attacked so many times for speaking out. Even those close to me have shouted at me in the street, called me names and said I'm looking for attention. I will speak my truth, I will share my experience as a Magdalene survivor, because Ireland still holds as dear as ever so many of the ideals that landed me there.

I owe nobody silence. You can tell your story, let me tell mine.

We worked from six in the morning, scrubbing and cleaning the convent, church and laundry, and then we went to Mass. After that we would have breakfast, something like bread and dripping, which made me gag, or watery porridge with no sugar, which didn't fill you, and then we would work in the laundry until dinner time, which going by the Angelus was at half past twelve. There were no clocks in New Ross. Then back to the laundry all day until teatime, which was around six.

Other Magdalene survivors will tell you the food given to the women was terrible, and I have no doubt it was, but for this poor child from Carlow who never got much at home other than bread and a scrape of an Oxo cube, I thought the food was good, although the portions were miserable. The smell of it would always perfume the air for about an hour in advance and I'd be working so hard that by the time it closed in on dinner or teatime, my mouth would be watering. There were stews, mutton or beef, cooked for hours with onions and carrots, served with big potatoes in a bowl that you'd peel yourself. You might get bacon and cabbage but never with sauce. There was fish on Fridays, with boiled potatoes. There'd be tea served from large kettles. The milk was already added.

You got dessert on a Sunday, bread pudding or stewed apples from the orchards.

In the laundry they took in washing from every institution around. There were big items – sheets, linens from the hotels, and heavy clothes, police and army uniforms and priests' or nuns' habits – and those were put through the machines. The smaller items, the 'delicates' as they were called, were hand-washed.

We all had our station and that was it. I worked the calendar for my whole time in New Ross and the same women always worked with me: Anna and Teresa. There was no change up. The days were monotonous toil, sheets coming through to me non-stop, one after the other. We were women with muscular arms from pulling sheets and dragging buckets. The only sounds were the movements against the material, the turning handles and machines going. There was no banter or chat like you would normally get when people are working together. It was hell.

The nuns stood at various points, changing guard now and again, keeping watch for bad behaviour. And anything other than doing the labour was bad behaviour.

The older women, who had clearly been there for years and years, were resigned to this job. But I was not, not ever. I was frustrated and upset. All the time. I was bored, I was worn out and every now and again, like the first time, I would lose it and kick up a fuss. I was only a child. It was normal.

When that happened, I would be given an awful job. Washing the nuns' knickers.

They'd be stacked up in a bucket, a month's worth of soiled underwear and sanitary napkins. I knew nothing about that, not at that age. I was too small to have a period and nobody had ever told me the facts of life. I suppose I'd have learned about it from other girls in school as I got a bit older, that was usually how it went. But in the convent nobody spoke anyway, let alone about those kinds of things.

Maybe all kids do this, but when I was there, when I didn't have an answer and couldn't ask the question, I just made up an answer. For this predicament I came to the conclusion that these bloody rags were from killing animals, maybe rats or kittens. That's what I went with.

That job made me sick. From the moment I dipped the first pair of pants into the water to start the handwashing, I would be retching and heaving the whole time. Usually there would be a washboard and maybe another woman to help me, and we would scrub the knickers and pads clean in cold water to shift the blood. It was a hard job and we used strong soap, the kind that stings your skin. The water turned grey quickly, like our bath at home, and there would be pubic hairs floating in it. They stuck to my hands; it was revolting.

I retched every time. The first time, the supervising nun lifted from her seat, her eyebrows shot up and she asked, 'Frances, are you sick?'

I nodded, let out my breath and stood up shaking my head, 'I can't do it. I can't wash them things.'

'You'll do the work you're given!' the nun said sternly.

The little woman working with me reached out and lifted

my hand from the water. She caught my eye and gently shook her head, taking my other hand away and placing both on top of the washboard. I held them there and she did all the scrubbing back and forth. I was so grateful for that.

That woman was Teresa. It hurts me that I don't know her real name. I don't know if she stayed there in New Ross or ever got out. At the time I thought she was probably a hundred, but she was maybe only in her sixties. Down in that laundry there was no make-up or hair dye, and women were just stripped to the basics. She was bent over at the shoulders like a crochet hook and was as thin as one, with little straight legs that were mottled around the shins. She had skin on her hands that was so thin from years of work that they looked like wax paper. I knew her hands really well.

They were helping hands.

In the recreation room her hands would find mine, struggling and shaky, and steady them, guiding my beads on one by one until I got the hang of it again. She would pat my hand if I fell asleep, in that funny way children do – mid-action – and brush my hair from my bleary eyes. In the dining room her hands would find mine under the table and pass me her portion of bread. She sometimes whispered, 'You're too thin,' as she passed it.

In the laundry, or hallway, or in Mass, her hand would shake me from a trance as a nun approached or pointed my way from afar.

I loved her hands – they were warm and soft and they looked like Granny's. They felt like Granny's. She asked me early on, one morning as we were paired up for scrubbing the floors together, 'Frances, what are you here for?'

I told her my name was Maureen.

She frowned when I said that. She asked me again, why was I in the asylum?

I said I didn't know.

She asked me where I slept and I told her in the dormitory with the schoolgirls.

'Why do you not go to school?' she asked.

'Silence!' came a nun's voice from somewhere.

I whispered that I didn't know, but I thought it was a mistake. I told her they stole my pencil case that my mammy gave me. I told her nobody would listen to me.

When I said that she threw the nuns daggers with her eyes.

It was the same nun who herded me back and forward to the dormitory through the tunnel. She was very young, with pink cheeks and big blue eyes that spent most of the time looking out the window. But don't let me romanticise her. She was a bitch like the rest of them.

That nun was called Mother John. I think she was the only nun whose name registered with me at all. That might be because I heard her name every night, 'Frances, go with Mother John.'

And for a long time, every night I would say, 'My name is Maureen.'

And for a long time, every night they would say, 'Well in this convent it's Frances. Don't answer back.'

Once I said to Mother John, as she skipped me across the corridors, down the tunnel and up the stairs, 'My father's name was John.'

She didn't reply to me and then I said, 'It's a boy's name.'

Silence.

'Are you a boy?' I asked. I meant it in good faith. I was trying to figure this out.

But all I got was a hard slap. She hit me in the back of the head and the force of it sent me onto my knees.

'Have some respect,' she said, picking me up by twisting my arm, and then dragged me along to the dormitory.

It was Mother John who warned me never to speak to the other children, never to open my mouth to them.

'Don't you even look at them,' she said.

I longed to speak to them. I often thought about waking one of them up and asking them if they wanted to play with me. But I never did speak to any of them – except for that once. And I paid for that, losing any contact with the other children for good.

I was in New Ross for more than two years and I couldn't tell you much about any of the nuns. Not even Mother John, and I spent the most time with her.

There was the watcher – the plump one who sat watching us in the laundry waiting for us to make mistakes so she could ram her crucifix into our ribs. There was the one who oversaw the factory line in recreation and kept us in stock of beads and wire, or wool and needles, to get the orders out. There was the one who took my pencil case, who I think was the Mother Superior, though all Good Shepherd nuns are called Mother, not Sister as you'd expect.

Mother. How ironic. Especially for that one. The more I asked the more violent she got.

'Can I have my pencil case? When am I going to school?'

Eventually, as I continued to ask, I would get beaten, punched right in the chest, sending my heart into my ribs and the wind out of me. But I still asked, and so she would beat me harder. It was a battle of wills. My will to be free and her will to break me. We were Samson and Goliath, but I am not sure who was who.

Years later I saw that they had recorded me in the convent records as 'troublesome'. When I saw that, in my late fifties, after years of trying to get them to admit I was there at all, it really hurt me through and through. I felt completely destroyed by that word. I was a little child. I'd been raped and abused, I was confused and imprisoned, and they looked at me in my situation and thought I was troublesome. As an adult, I imagine travelling back in time to knock on the door and take those harridans, those evil bitches, to task over the terrified little girl they had on her hands and knees scrubbing their floors and burning her hands in their laundry.

What absolute devils they all were. Every single one of them.

Troublesome, they called me.

That has hurt me more, I think, than anything else.

26

NITS

The first I knew about having nits in the laundry was an itchy head that attracted the attention of one of the nuns who took one look at my scalp and shouted, 'Mother, her head is walking!'

I was then dragged out of the laundry and down the hall to where the Mother Superior was. I don't remember who did the dragging because I was really feeling the intense itch all over my head that made me want to tear at my skull. The heat of the laundry, as soon as we started work, escalated the itch, and I was seen by the nun scratching between turns of the calendar handle. She had taken one look at my hair and pulled me out of there.

The Mother Superior took a long look at me and rolled her eyes.

'Get her back to work as soon as it's done,' she said, and I was dragged back down the hall to a small washroom area near the laundry.

Within minutes I was on my knees over newspaper and they were shaving my head.

When I tell people that, they often nod and show concern of course. Having your head shaved is humiliating, but the word 'shaved' doesn't really cover what the nuns did to us at all. People think of an electric razor and a gentle buzzing on the scalp, with hair falling away like leaves, like you'd see in military films.

But in Magdalene laundries every opportunity to punish us was taken up with gusto, and no chance to hurt us was lost. I think options were taken to make us suffer more. So when I had head lice, and the solution was to shave my head, they did that with scissors – the kind you see sheep shorn with. They pulled the hair up and slipped the blades of the scissors to the very base and cut. And often they cut through the skin, pulled up with the hair. It was painful and horrible and so cruel.

I screamed my head off as they did that to me. I was being shorn like a sheep. My hair was cut to the scalp and there was stinging stabbing pains as the scissors cut through me. Trickles of blood tickled my neck. Then they ducked me over a basin and poured some foul-smelling chemicals onto my damaged scalp. I screamed so hard I hurt my throat.

They were brutes. I know the nuns who did that to me are rotting in hell.

After that, they left me. So I washed my scalp as best I could. The soap stung, but the water was cooling against the fire of the chemicals they'd applied. Then I dried it. There were no mirrors in the laundry. What would we need them for?

Beside the door there was an image in a frame. It was the face of Jesus Christ, a crown of thorns pushed down onto his scalp. Blood ran down his forehead, onto his face. People are often punished for the sins of others.

I wiped a trickle of my own blood where it had run to the end of my nose, and stood there.

Another nun popped her head in the door and looked at me and left. I heard her footsteps rushing up the corridor. She returned with the nun who had done the shearing and they were arguing.

'She has her Confirmation Mass on Sunday,' the concerned nun said to the shearer.

Another nun ran in, eyes wide, and her hands flew up to her mouth. 'She has her Confirmation,' she said through them.

'Well nobody told me!' the shearer said. 'She has lice!'

'Stay there,' one of them said to me and they all left. I shoved myself under the sinks, cradling my head, trying to get away from the stabbing pain of my own scalp. My throat was raw from screaming and I had a headache.

The Mother Superior returned with them.

'Frances,' she said, 'come out of there.'

I crawled out and stood up, holding onto my head with both arms. The Mother Superior pulled my arms away and let out an exasperated sigh when she saw the good work of the nuns.

'We can't have her like this at the Confirmation,' she said. 'I've already had two calls from Mrs Ryan about this one.'

The shearer grovelled. 'I have a veil. We can put her in a veil.' She ran off and returned with it, waving it in the air, and as soon as she reached me, plopped it onto my head.

The Mother Superior rolled her eyes, 'It's ghoulish,' she said.

The shearer grovelled more. 'We can put a hat on, Mother, we have some in St Aidan's.'

With my head tonsured I returned to work. My eyes met sorry eyes. My fellow inmates had compassion. That was where the warmth was in that place, in the unspoken understanding of the other women. They knew what I was going through. Only they did.

**

I don't remember the day much. Nobody I loved came down to New Ross to watch me make my Confirmation, but I think a suit was sent down. Miss Emily and I walked down to the church and I had a straw hat covering my scabbed head. It was pulled down as far as it would go. The veil was abandoned and I was left like that, bald under a hat.

I felt something walking to the church in the sunshine, I do remember that. A feeling of interest that I hadn't felt in so long, looking at the other kids and the adults all buzzing around the front of the church.

All the children from St Aidan's seemed to have their families around them. I saw fathers and mothers and siblings, all happy with the day out. I imagined my own mother and granny, down with Michael and Paddy, coming around the corner in their Sunday best, and I wished it could be. I knew my mother had sent down the suit I was wearing – perhaps Sister Cecilia had it in the convent – and it gave me comfort to wear it.

Nobody hanselled me that day with a coin or two, like I saw with the other kids. Nobody wished me well or asked me if I was enjoying myself. I was brought in, confirmed with everyone else, and back to work I went.

But it was a break from the monotony. I enjoyed it.

27

THE DUBLIN GIRL

There are two women who I think about often. One of those was the Dublin girl. I don't remember her name or the name she was given, because she wasn't there for long.

They dragged her into the convent. At one point the driver and two nuns had her by the arms and legs and were pulling her over the tiles to the laundry. She was crying and wailing and kicking as she pulled at their hands and tried to free herself.

'Lemme alone yiz wretches, lemme alone!'

I knew that accent.

I was really interested in this new one – she was young, maybe sixteen or seventeen, and I thought she looked like a movie star. Her hair was black and it fell down her back in waves. The first thing they did was cut it off as she howled, and if she kicked out or tried to stop them, they would beat her into submission. It was hard to watch, even though I had seen women beaten so many times – this girl took so long to give in, I was really upset by it. They cut it all off and left her heaving with sobs, sitting on the floor with a shorn and bleeding head. Her face was in her hands and the spasm of her lungs as they attempted to balance the oxygen in and out sounded so painful.

She was put straight to work, standing near me to fold the sheets as I fed sheets into the calendar. She stared at me. 'You're only a babby,' she said, and her breath hitched. I said nothing.

Her breathing settled eventually, and I kept hearing her tell herself the same thing over and over, 'He'll come ta get me, he will,' and she kept touching her tonsured head and flinching with the pain.

Over the next few days she was broken down – like we had all been. She made a run for the door the first day – the one where laundry would be taken in and out – and the nuns absolutely thrashed her. She fought them though, tooth and nail, like a wild cat. But she was no match for them. None of us were.

'Do none of yiz talk in here or wha?' she said loudly to the room and giggled in this husky, high-pitched way that warmed the room instantly. I loved the sound of it. I wanted to hear it again.

'Silence!' the watcher called out.

'No chance of a radio, Sister?' she said.

The watcher started to get down off her perch and I wanted to warn the girl, but I couldn't speak. So I just shook my head.

'This place is dull,' she said, but the watcher had crossed the room and punched the girl in the ribs.

She tried to protest, but she was punched again.

'Do not speak. Work!' the nun said.

She made a proper run for it then, a few days later. I noticed she wasn't in the laundry when we were working and I wasn't sure where she was, but I'd so much work ahead of me I just got on with it. The nuns seemed distracted though. They kept leaving the room and changing guard more often than we were used to. I heard the gate opening more than normal and at one point I saw a policeman come through it in his navy uniform and speak to one of the nuns in the courtyard there. It was obvious something was going on, and through looks and whispers it came through to me that the Dublin girl had escaped. I'd no idea how or when, but she was gone.

They brought her back the next morning. We heard the screams of her down the corridors where we were scrubbing. She was howling the convent down, like an animal being brought to slaughter. She didn't want to be here. She was being held against her will. We saw her again at dinner. I caught and held her eye and she was crying silently the whole time. There were cuts and bruising on her jaw and on her arms. The nuns had showed her their might, there was no doubt about it.

Then, another day, she was working with me again. But she was hit so much those first few days that she was utterly defeated. The girl who had been brought in fighting was gone. There was no fight now.

We were put together a good bit then, especially for the cleaning job on Saturday, when we were sent upstairs in the convent to clean the nuns' corridors. Those corridors had carpet on them, to muffle footsteps I'd imagine.

The bedrooms always surprised me. With all the drama of the convent itself, with its statues and ornaments, the bedrooms were so basic. They were cells. Tiny square rooms with a single iron bed, always immaculately laid with blankets folded under a white sheet. There were frames on the wall, but no warm smiling faces of family or friends, just a dying Jesus or praying pope.

What choice did nuns make? And for what? I wonder did they ever regret it, in the middle of the night in that little room, and cry for the life they could have had? Is that what was wrong with them? Is that why they hit me so hard? Because they knew I would be free someday and they would die there? Is that why they wanted us to die there too?

Our lady, the Virgin Mary, was everywhere in the convent. Huge statues in the church and the halls. There was a statue in each of the nuns' cells too. We would rub the dust off them with our rags and clean them each week.

'Virgin, my eye,' the Dublin girl said that week. I didn't know what she meant, so I just shrugged.

'How old are you?' she asked me.

'I think I'm thirteen or nearly,' I whispered. Even though there were no nuns around I didn't want to talk just in case I got a beating.

'Jaysus, I thought you were younger than that,' she said. 'And are you pregnant?'

I was a child who thought babies came from the hospital. Even at twelve, I really thought that my mother went down to the hospital and a nurse gave her a baby. I had no reason to think my mother was lying when she told me that, and nobody had ever mentioned anything else to me, so that was the truth as far as I understood it. I didn't really know what pregnant was.

I must have shown it on my face.

She said, 'Do you not know where babies come from?' and did that giggle again that I loved so much.

'I do so,' I said, but I was beginning to think I might not.

The Dublin girl pulled her dress tight over her tummy; it was high and rounded.

'They come from women,' she said. 'I have one inside my belly right now.'

I did not know what to think.

'Did you not know that?' she said and I shook my head. I did not.

'Well,' she said and she leaned in and told me the entire process. She told me everything there was to know about the making of babies and their births, and that Dublin girl shocked the life out of me.

She knew she had. She ruffled my hair and said, 'Don't be worrying about it, you're too young for any of that anyway.'

Of course, she didn't know what I had been through. She had no way to know that my mind was racing and I was trying to make sense of things I had been through in light of this new information.

We started on the next room. There was trousers folded on the chair in that one. The Dublin girl started laughing as she moved them to clean the chair. She was giggling away and she kept saying to me, 'Are you getting it?' as she folded and refolded those trousers. I was not getting it. I do now.

The following morning after that the Dublin girl was gone. I never saw her again.

***

The other woman I think about a lot, especially as I get older myself, was the old Magdalene woman called Annie. She worked alongside me in the laundry and in my memory she was as old as Granny, so probably in her seventies or eighties. She was completely institutionalised. She often carried a rolled-up cloth, a small blanket, in her arms as if it was a baby and the nuns never seemed to care much, they just let her wander around most of the time. She was so old, what could they have done? She would bounce the bundle of nothing in her arms back and forth, until she would be told to get back to work, and she would lay it down somewhere as carefully as though it were a sleeping baby and start work again.

There were a few women like that there in New Ross. Really old women who had lost the reality around them and lived in a daze. They rarely spoke, rarely did anything other than the monotonous movements they were permitted to, scrubbing or cleaning, barely eating. Years of malnutrition and hard labour had reduced them to walking bones. Even at twelve and thirteen I knew that what had been done to them, their incarceration, was the reason why they were so strange. It terrified me. I imagined myself still there as an old woman, my whole life gone because of a man's actions.

One day when we were working Annie slowed right down and the nun called out to her to 'get back to it' but Annie didn't. She slumped a little at her station, her shoulders fell forward and she looked so grey I stopped what I was doing and watched her. The lady across from her reached over and touched her, and when she did Annie slid down the machine she was working at and sat on the floor.

I was horrified. I heard the swish of the watcher as she climbed off her perch and made her way furiously across the laundry.

'What are you doing, Annie?' she said. 'Get up!'

The old woman shook her head. I saw a tear pool in her eye and slide down her face.

The nun pulled her hair, yanked her face to meet her eyes and the moment she did I saw the nun's eyebrows flash up as her mouth dropped open and she screamed, 'BACK TO WORK!' to all of us, and then she took old Annie by the back of her dress and pulled her out of the room.

I went to follow them with Annie's little bundle – she never went anywhere without it and she used to cry if she couldn't find it – but I was stopped at the door. I saw the nuns carry her by the legs and arms into the convent.

We never saw Annie again. She isn't listed on any of the graves of New Ross, so I'm not sure what happened to her, and because I didn't know her real name I can never find out. That incident plays on my mind still. The frustration of hearing a commotion in the corridor, the banging of doors and the furious squeaks of the nuns' shoes as they dealt with whatever it was that was happening, it got in. I wanted to know what happened to Annie. I still do.

28

VISITORS

On my records it states that I was sent home for Christmas. I can tell you, hand on heart, that never happened. I was kept at the convent at Christmas and except for the fact that the laundry did not open that day, it was the same routine. My mother sent me a box that first year, which I was given, after the nuns had gone through it, of course, for the good chocolate.

In the box there was a bottle of holy water, a packet of Smarties and a set of Rosary beads. They were the exact same beads we used in the convent. I wanted to smash them, but instead I just popped them into my tin at recreation and took things a little slower that night.

My mother did visit me in New Ross once. It was so far from Carlow in those days, and she would have had to find a lift there and back, so it usually wasn't possible. But she did come at least once that I remember and sat in the visitors' room waiting while I was called for. I'd been told that morning that I had a visitor expected, but then I was ignored all day and nobody appeared and so I thought maybe I had misheard. When they finally called me after dinner to see her, I almost didn't want to go.

I was glad I did, because my oldest brother, Michael, was with her, home for a visit from Artane. It was a strange moment to see him. The face I had always known looked so different, so thin and tired, and I'd imagine he saw mine that way too. We just stood and looked at each other and said nothing. Then the nun who supervised the visit told us all to sit down at a table where they had put flowers and where a younger nun put a teapot with cups and saucers on it, and a plate of biscuits.

My mother spoke to me like we were in a play. 'How are you, Maureen?' she said. I loved the sound of my name from her mouth. It was like it echoed off the walls, that forbidden name.

'You look very pale,' she said. 'Have you lost weight?'

I didn't answer. I just nodded. Sure, first of all I wouldn't know. There wasn't a mirror in New Ross. But second of all, there was no point in speaking. The nuns were sitting there like wardens so I couldn't speak the truth. My mother thought I was going to school here. That was obvious from the things she asked, and I didn't want to lie. But I didn't think I could explain, so I didn't speak. The nuns answered for me, mostly. I could see that made Michael's mouth twitch. He knew.

My mother was drinking with the saucer held under her cup. She held it with such a dainty hand and I tried to copy her, lifting my cup with two fingers, but I wobbled and spilt it onto the table. I was surprised not to get a crucifix in the ribs, but it was just wiped away by the nun without a word. This was a show.

'Maureen,' my mother said, 'will you be careful, please?' She smiled at the nun apologetically.

'It's Frances, Mammy,' I said.

'Who is Frances?' she asked, and I pointed at myself.

'My name here is Frances,' I said. 'I'm not allowed be called Maureen here.'

'Why not?' she said.

I shrugged. 'I don't know, but that's how it is,' I said.

My mother looked perturbed. Michael cleared his throat and shook his head. He got it.

But my mother wracked her brains for a good reason – she would always forgive nuns and priests, always came up with excuses.

'It must be for your Confirmation,' she said.

I knew that wasn't it, but I didn't say anything else. What was the point?

So I just asked after Paddy.

'He lives up with Granny now,' Michael said, and gave me a little grin of empathy. He knew how hard that would be to hear.

I was happy to hear it, but also felt my own heart break. I wanted my brother safe of course, but I was filled with a desperate wish to be there too.

We didn't say much else, not my mother or Michael or me. I won't say there was unspoken communication. There was nothing much passing between us at all. We were three worn-out animals in the same vicinity.

When they left I remember feeling relief that I could just go back to my silent routine. Watching my mother under pressure to make small talk, and making small talk myself, was exhausting.

But, on the other hand, I longed to climb out the window and race after them. I still find it impossible to think how I would have put up with abuse at home over the work in the laundry. I never had enough to eat in Roncalli Place, I slept with others in cramped uncomfortable beds and I was abused. But I would have taken it all just to see my granny. I missed her the most of all.

***

There was a woman who used to come to visit the nuns in New Ross, and she would always make a point of coming in to see the women when she did. Mrs Ryan was elderly, a local, and was a direct relation – a cousin – to the recently murdered president John F. Kennedy. This made her a sort of celebrity in the community, more so since he was dead, and there would be great ceremony when she came to the convent each time. On his visit to Ireland, he had spent much time with her, and so she had become a dignitary of sorts, by proxy. When she came, she was made very welcome and she always brought a tin of sweets for the 'penitents', which she would make a point of telling us about and showing to us when she was brought in.

'Aren't you all working so hard?' she would say. 'I hope you get lots of breaks.'

The nuns would confidently talk about the break for Mass and our 'wonderful recreation' time, which satisfied her. Little did she know. She would wave at us as she left, tell us to enjoy the tin of whatever she had brought.

Those chocolates rarely made it to us. The nuns kept good chocolates, Cadbury's or the like, for themselves. Nothing would ever appear for us if it was a good brand. But when the sweets she brought weren't to their taste, we might see the tin appear at teatime and it would be passed around with strict instructions to take one. Of course, I took two. I was a teenager. It was to be expected. When my friends talk about their rebellious teenage years, sneaking in and out of windows to the local dance, rolling their skirts up past their knee on the way home from school, kissing boys in the bushes ... I think about my own teenage rebellions ... slowing down while stringing rosaries, mouthing prayers and not actually saying them, and taking two sweets at dinner. I took one to eat now and tucked the other in the sleeve of my cardigan to suck when I got into bed. Sugar was so rare.

I remember on one of the occasions that the late American president's cousin came to visit she asked the nuns in front of us all where we went on excursions.

'Where do the ladies get days out to?'

The nun began to explain that the laundry runs every day, but Mrs Ryan interrupted her. 'Now please, Mother,' she said, 'everyone needs a day out from time to time.'

The nuns fobbed it off with a distraction, but the next evening we were told just after dinner that we were to have an outing to the beach the following day.

We were given the information by a nun with a sober face and a deep frown, and so I wasn't sure I had heard her correctly, given that she looked like she was giving us bad news. I suppose it was bad for them – they'd miss a day of laundry over it and lose the money.

The next morning a coach pulled up at the archway and instead of filing into the laundry after Mass we filed on board, and sat in twos all the way to a long and quiet beach in Wexford.

I was a child from Carlow. I had never seen a beach.

**

High white dunes with sharp grass pressed up out of the tarmac in the empty car park and there was a smell of salt and heat in the air. It was midweek, and where normally the beach would be a cacophony of children's screams and voices in excitement in the water, that day it was quiet but for one or two walkers along the shore. As we filed off the bus we queued up at the public toilet, and when relieved of that burden, we walked along the well-worn pathway though the dunes to the beach. Sand filled my shoes immediately.

I was surprised at the extent of the sea. It stretched away to the horizon forever. I sat and stared at it. The breeze was cold and cut through me, but I was entranced by the ever-moving water. Most of the women paddled and splashed in the water. Who knows when they had been outside before – some of them had been living at the laundry for many years. It was a strange dynamic; we were so used to not speaking that nobody did, even here. Even sitting there on a white, sandy beach in the sun we were mostly silent. I started to feel the cold and complained, mostly to myself under my breath, that I wanted to go back on the bus. I had really liked the bus. The seat was comfortable and I enjoyed looking out the window.

Sandwiches were handed out, which kept me quiet for a while – they were ham and butter – and there was tea poured from huge flasks. It was warming and for a moment I was content. One of the women coaxed me to the water's edge, coerced me to take off my shoes and socks, and then pulled me in to paddle in the water. She held my hand, but I didn't last a minute. I hadn't forgotten the pain of my near-drowning in the river in Bennekerry.

So I sat a little away from the others, in a nook in the dunes where the breeze couldn't get me. I watched the women paddle and splash, and saw, in the bursts of laughter and their smiles, hints of the people they might have been before they were institutionalised and restricted. I looked at the way the sun made dancing lights on the water. I saw the water cover the shore and retreat over and over again. I watched the grass moving in the breeze. A gull hovered in the sky above me and then flew away.

I closed my eyes and imagined I could fly away too.

29

TRAFFICKED

'But where am I going?'

I asked that question over and over again. I had been woken up before the other women, and made to wash and dress, and when I came back out, I noticed the nun had my little suitcase tied up. I thought I might be going home, so I asked, but she didn't say. They fed me a few pieces of bread and butter. Then she stood me outside the convent, in the small yard, to wait.

'Who am I waiting for?' I said. 'Where am I going?'

'You'll see when you get there,' was the final answer.

'Can I have my pencil case?' I didn't want to leave without it.

The question was met with a dramatic roll of the nun's eyes. That harmless wooden box, it meant so much to me and they knew it. In a way I think I put my soul inside that box on the way to New Ross and that is why I was so desperate to get it back. It was my totem, perhaps. Something that represented independence, future, self, and something that was given to me with love. So when they took it, and refused to tell me why or where it was, I lost more than the thing itself. It might sound strange, but it's how I feel. It was everything to me, that pencil case. It was a symbol of my freedom. And at the end of the day, in Carlow I may have been hurting, but I was free.

When they took that pencil case, they took everything: my name, my education, my rights. I left my soul inside that box and they left me with nothing.

I'm not sure I ever really got my soul back.

A Morris Minor pulled up with a well-dressed gentleman behind the wheel. He spoke to the nun and she gave him an envelope, and I got into the car.

He was just lifting his foot off the clutch and the car was moving forward on its wheels when I yelped and shouted, 'Wait, stop!'

He stood on the brake and we both bucketed forward, but I rolled down my window and shouted back at the nun, 'I'll be back here!' I yelled at her. 'You know I'll come back here!' And I waved my fist.

It was a prophecy.

I was preoccupied and scared for the first part of the journey, trying to take in the signs as we passed to figure out if we were headed for Carlow, as I hoped.

'Where are we going?' I said.

'That way,' said the driver, pointing forward as a joke, but I didn't laugh. I knew he was avoiding the question, and that wasn't funny.

The car was a novelty, with shiny silver chrome on the dash and red leather seats that were comfortable against my thin body. I eventually relaxed into them and looked out the window at Ireland passing by, the sheep and fields and houses, and I felt a small freedom out there. I cranked the window and felt the air on my face. I let out a long sigh and the driver was amused. He patted me on the head and asked me, 'Are you okay? Are you alright? Nearly there.'

I have no idea who that man was. That trafficker of child slaves from one county to the other. At the end of the day that is exactly what he was doing. He must have known what I was coming from and where I was going.

Eventually that Morris Minor pulled up to St Michael's Convent of Mercy in Athy, County Kildare. It was a huge stone building with gardens that looked like something from a fairy tale. And like most fairy tales, there was evil lurking behind the roses.

The moment I saw St Michael's my stomach dropped with the deepest anxiety. I wasn't going home, I was going to work here. The atmosphere was dark and grim, despite the flowers blooming along the drive.

We got out of the car and the man walked me up to the door with my suitcase in his hand. He knocked. His knock was answered by a thin young nun wearing black and white. She didn't say anything, just moved away from the door so we could come in, and then we followed her up a hallway to a reception room. She took my suitcase and opened it on the table, using her finger to move the top layer to expose my pants and vests underneath. I was embarrassed because the man was standing right there.

'Not much with you,' the nun said, which I didn't understand, though I felt humiliated anyway. I wanted to tell her about my pencil case. I wanted to shout that they took everything I had in New Ross. I wanted to bellow like a bull into her grey face that

I wanted my fucking pencil case back. But, of course, I didn't. I swallowed the lump in my throat and calmed the growing panic that I was feeling. Having left New Ross, now I was here and I didn't know why. I reached across and covered up my exposed underwear. Then I put my eyes on the ground, and to be honest I'm not sure I ever lifted them again for years.

***

St Michael's Convent in Athy was run by the Sisters of Mercy. They recorded my date of birth in their records on my arrival as being in my 'fourteenth year'. It's vague, most likely because I was still thirteen. I'd been in St Mary's in New Ross for two years. I'd served that time there and I would serve the same again here, only I didn't know it then.

St Michael's was much smaller, and the numbers of women were less, maybe thirty max. There must have been fifty in New Ross by the time I left, if not more. The workroom in Athy was smaller, the equipment was smaller, and the amount of laundry was less, but we worked just as hard. It was one of the Magdalene laundries that presented itself to society as a 'training school' where girls could go to learn the art of domestic service in order to find a job. There were a few laundries that dressed up their title that way, but they were the same slave camps as any of them. Not one of us learned anything other than how to work in a laundry till we dropped, just like the others. I spent my days in St Michael's doing laundry, scrubbing and cleaning. Without pay.

By the time I left New Ross and went to Athy I was already a broken person. I didn't rebel there at all, I asked nothing, I kept my head down and got on with it. I didn't annoy the nuns with repetitive questions. I had given up. I did my work, ate and went to bed. I avoided punishment. I abandoned all ideas I had of who I was or what I thought. I said nothing.

As a result of that I have few memories, though I think that's the same for all of us – it is only events that stand out and I had none of those. I don't remember the inmates there, and I don't remember the nuns. I have few stories about St Michael's.

We were given orders in the morning, spoken to sharply as if we were incapable of understanding. We were always shouted at, barked at in the laundries. There was no reason for that – speaking kindly would have cost the nuns nothing.

Even with the smaller loads in Athy, and the smaller machines, the work was harder. There was more bending and more heaving and pulling wet laundry than you'd have in New Ross. It was also a place where we had contact with the public, who would drop in their laundry.

There was no calendar in this new laundry, but there was a huge steam press. I was given the never-ending job of pressing the starched clothes. Starch isn't common these days, but it was normal then to mix starch powder with water to form a loose jelly that you would dip clothes into, then wring the mixture out and hang them up to dry. Just before they were fully dry you would press them, almost to set the starch into the cloth.

That starch and me, we were not friends. My skin reacted to the mix by breaking out in dermatitis, small splits in my over-dried skin that left my hands raw every day. And there was no break from the work to let it heal, so I lived with that every day. I was in constant pain. And on top of that, working the press meant I burned myself regularly. The machines were designed to be used by fully-grown adults not small-sized children, and it was difficult for me to avoid the steam as I held the corners of the clothes to get the right fold without making dents in the fabric. Marks were not tolerated.

One morning there I was working really slowly, as I had open sores on my knuckles and also a case of something like tendonitis in my elbow, so I couldn't fold well. I was going easy, but not voluntarily – I couldn't physically go faster.

Suddenly I heard a sound and the corner of my eye was lashed with something. It felt like a bee sting and my hand flew up expecting to find a pulsing stinger on my cheek. But then again, the same lash on my cheek. I whipped my head around. The supervising nun, the old harridan, was whipping me with the end of a wet pillowcase that she had picked up off the pile next to me.

I gasped and put my hand up, but she flicked it again and caught me across the bottom lip.

'Stop!' I cried out.

'Work!' she said, and I got straight back to it, faster than before even though it was intensely painful. My lesson was learned faster there than it had been in New Ross.

That flick became familiar in Athy. If you stopped to rub your neck, or shoulders, you'd hear it and flinch just as it reached your skin. Sometimes you wouldn't be able to work out why you got it and you'd fidget around, changing your position, your hands going faster, higher, until it stopped. Some of us would respond with tears, some with yelps and some – like me – would show no reaction if we could help it. God love us. Training school my eye.

***

The Mother Superior of the convent in Athy was rarely seen in the laundry, unlike the head nun in New Ross, who liked nothing more than coming down on us like thunder. This nun kept to the main building of the convent and ignored the chain gang working to death in the laundry. The only time we saw her was when she would do the rounds during recreation time to check the quality of our work.

In Athy the main product we made was Aran sweaters. I often wondered if the people who bought those jumpers had any idea of the suffering that went into them. It used to cross my mind how suffering is promoted as a way to a good life by the Church, and I'd think isn't that the biggest con of the century. Because to me it always looked as though the ones at the top weren't suffering much at all.

The dormitories in Athy were smaller than New Ross – I was sharing with maybe ten or twelve others – and whereas most of the women in New Ross were old, here they were mostly in their twenties and thirties. There were no old ladies at all. Just young women who looked old, with shorn hair.

My mother came once as Athy was close and she managed to get a lift. We talked for a while, very politely.

'Oh!' She said suddenly and rummaged in her bag, pulling out one of those thin, flat Dairy Milk bars you don't see anymore.

'Your granny sent you that up,' she said and I took it from where she slid it over the table.

It was a reminder of the big bar in Sharkey's – I knew it and that made me smile.

I didn't want to ask, but I did. 'How is Granny?'

'Well, your granny misses you something fierce, girl,' my

mother told me. 'She's always going on. Won't let up to bring you back,' she said.

I was touched, but I swallowed all my emotions as best I could. I missed my granny.

'I tell her you're getting your education,' my mother said. 'She is proud of that.'

I wanted to cry. I wasn't getting anything but hit and slapped and overworked and treated like a slave, but I held my tears back.

When I recovered, I said, 'Tell Granny I miss her. Tell her I miss her so much.' The muscles in my chin pulled in and I breathed in and out to calm myself. I didn't want to cry.

I saw something cross my mother's face, regret perhaps that it was my grandmother I missed that much and not her. I did miss my mother, but there was never time for love or affection in her home – she had too much to do and too many of us.

The nun began to clear the table as we sat there and my mother made small talk about prayers and good turns that she thought would impress these holy women. I watched the chocolate bar being lifted onto a tray and carried out by one of them, with the empty cups and saucers. I told myself I'd get it at dinner time, the way we sometimes got a biscuit. But I never did. I lay in bed for many nights imagining them choking to death on it, those hypocrites. No wonder they were all fat.

I knew the days of the week by what tasks I would work on in Athy, and it was easier to bear than the seven-day repetition of New Ross. If I was on polishing the silver, I knew it was a Saturday; if I was scrubbing the corridors in the nuns' quarters I knew it was Sunday. To be honest it didn't matter, because we never had a minute off, but the days of the week having a variety of work made it a little easier. I didn't bother with anyone there. I wasn't interested. I was too tired to smile or interact, and most others were the same. I wondered had we all come from other places, we were all so worn out. Any familiarity you showed to anyone in there, you'd be separated, so even in our rooms at night we kept ourselves to ourselves. And when we did interact, we were rude to each other. We snapped back. Questions were answered with 'Find out yourself' or 'Leave me alone' and other rudeness like that. We didn't want to be friendly.

Sometimes the younger ones, me and one or two other teens, were sent upstairs and told to be quiet and stay up there until we were fetched. The men in the suits would come. We would see them out the window and we knew we weren't supposed to be there either. I don't believe the state would have done one thing about us even if they had seen us.

***

I'd thought I had encountered the most revolting job in New Ross, with the nuns' undergarments. But unfortunately, for me, there was a worse one.

In those days people didn't use disposable hankies like you see now. They carried a square of hemmed cotton around in their sleeve to use during the day. And those squares, small chequered ones and larger white ones, as used by the nuns and priests of Athy, came to the laundry to be washed. And I was the poor unfortunate who was made do it.

Buckets full of steeping hankies would be delivered to my station every single day. I never ever got used to it. I would have to reach in to remove them, rinse and scrub them and wring them out when clean. Scrubbing them against the washboards had my stomach heaving, the lumps of green snot would catch on the ridges and fix themselves there, and large clumps of opaque mucus would float like egg whites in the water and stick to my fingers.

I absolutely hated that job. It made me physically retch. On one occasion it made me vomit, and I had to run through the laundry to the toilet to do it. The supervising nun saw me and came after me. 'What's wrong with you?' she said.

I lifted my head from the pan, green to the gills.

I hissed at her as to how I was not able. I said my stomach was weak, I couldn't take it. I told her it was disgusting. I begged to do anything else – I'd clean toilets, empty pans, anything.

'I can't wash them anymore, Sister,' I started bawling. 'It's making me puke. I can't do it. I can't.'

I vomited again. And again.

She waited for my retching to finish and dragged me off to see the Mother Superior.

I stood there, sweating and clearly ill, and was told, 'Frances, you'll do those hankies.'

'She got sick, Mother,' the nun told her. 'She has a weak stomach. Should she do something else?'

'No, no,' the Mother Superior said, and my stomach turned, 'she will do the hankies.'

The next day when the bucket was placed at my feet, I upended it. I didn't plan to, but I picked it up by the edges and threw it away from me, spilling its disgusting contents all over the floor. And I opened my mouth and screamed.

If you have ever seen a volcano erupt, imagine that, but with words. I cursed the heavens and sent myself to hell. I did not give one shit who heard me, I let it all out. I roared at God, at His son, at His mother – who were they to send me here? I wanted out. I wanted to hang off gates and kick stones. I wanted to run so fast I couldn't breathe. I wanted to hide in ditches with my brothers and laugh till we were sick. I wanted music and hopscotch and my Indian doll. I WANTED MY GRANNY.

'I don't want to work in this place, you shower of bastards. I hope you all go straight to hell. Fuck you all!' I sent the bucket flying with a kick. I noticed a hanky stuck to my leg and peeled it off and threw it. It hit one of my fellow workers.

'Sorry,' I said, and then let a roar out of me again. 'I'm not supposed to be here. I hate it here. I want my pencil case! I want my pencil case back, you thieves. You fecking stole it. I want it. I want my ... I want my pencil case ... my granny. I want my granny.'

I collapsed on the floor sobbing, only to rise up again with the same outburst, only louder and with more rage – the words were coming out as screams. I slapped my own face. I twisted my arms up and shook my fist at the dying Christ on the cross that hung in front of me.

'And as for you ... !!!' I shouted at him but didn't dare to finish.

I turned again to the nun. 'I'm not doing those FECKING HANKIES!!'

I kicked that bucket around the laundry, smacked my fists against the machines. I just went for it. I raged, I kicked, I screamed. I pulled my own hair and slapped my forehead. I pummelled the laundry, pulled at it, swung from it. I fell over and stood back up and then threw myself down again and kicked and kicked.

'I WANT MY PENCIL CASE, YOU THIEVING BASTARDS!' I screamed.

And they let me. Not one nun came near me. I don't know what would have happened had they. I might have clawed their eyes out, or bitten their faces.

When I wore myself out, screaming so long I lost my breath and had to roll onto my belly on the cold floor to catch it back, they coaxed me to the Reverend Mother's office, where it was clear that other nuns had already filled her in on the Medusa I had become twenty minutes before. One nun was crying in the corner, another had her Rosary beads around her fingers and was in some state of prayer.

I suppose I had been so well behaved until that moment that they just didn't know what they were looking at. It was, simply, the end of my tether.

'What's going on with this outburst, Frances?' the Reverend Mother asked me.

'I can't clean them hankies,' I said.

'I see ... but you are shouting about a pencil case, what pencil case? Did someone steal something?' She did look concerned.

I told her that story. 'Them nuns in New Ross took my pencil case my mammy gave to me and they didn't give it back. It's mine,' I said.

'I see ... I'll call the sisters and ask them to send it on, Frances,' she said. 'Now go and wash your face and go back to work.'

'I'm not doing them hankies, Mother,' I warned her.

She ignored that and waved me out. A nun kept me company as I washed my face.

When I got back to the laundry, the bucket of hankies had been refilled and was waiting at my station. I gave in.

Some time after that, I called into the Reverend Mother's office to ask about the phone call. She told me she had called and the sisters told her they couldn't find it.

'They're a pack of lying thieves then,' I said, knowing full well that there was no way to lose a pencil case in a convent.

'Frances, do not call the Good Shepherd Sisters names,' she warned.

'They're thieves. You're all thieves,' I was fuming.

Even with those two interactions, I think the Mother Superior and I were on good terms. When I left her after my couple of years, she told me I was 'pleasant'. I kept that word with me for many years.

30

TRAFFICKED AGAIN

I was in Athy for a couple of years. I know I was there two summers at least, when once again I found myself being trafficked to another laundry in another place. I presumed I was going back to New Ross the moment I was called out of the laundry and handed my small suitcase, packed for me and tied with string. But I ended up, after another journey with another strange man in a car, in Dublin, at St Mary's on the Merrion Road, the asylum for the blind.

On arrival I was taken by the unusual crucifix above the door of the building, on each side of which were two triangular windows with circular panes.

Inside the convent was light and brighter than the others, but I looked straight down the corridors at the tiles, making mental additions as to how long they would take to scrub. The corridors here were straight and had no bends. My heart sank at the length of them. Scrubbing a straight run was always harder because there was nothing to break it up.

***

I was given a tour of the convent by the trustee, Miss Hilary, that first day. I was shown where everything went and shown the laundry, and I was lifted a little by how bright and roomy it was. There was such a sense of calm that the other places didn't have. In comparison to the two other prisons I'd lived at, this one had warmth. As we passed the rooms – the dining room, the canteen, the library – I thought about the blind. I was curious about the library because I didn't know there were Braille books. And then I was shown the recreation room and I wondered what products we would make here. The Sisters of Charity who ran the convent looked like the Sisters of Mercy from Athy, wearing all black with a white box wimple around their cheeks. Their costumes were so impractical. A young nun ran down the stairs and skipped the last step with a smile, passing me by in a flurry. Her expression was so warm, I still think about that smile. It was the only real one I got in all my time with the institutions. That smile gave me hope for that place. The rest of the nuns I came across, in the years I was held prisoner, are a blur, but I remember that young nun's face like she just passed me now. I wonder what became of her – did she stay there until she was old, or did she leave and fly away like it always seemed she might?

***

In comparison to the other two laundries, the blind school was different. It was so light-filled and more open plan than the other convents. And because there were residents, it had something like the feel of a hotel about it. Miss Hilary told me if I had any issues, I was to come to her. But there was never any infighting, never trouble between the women, not there, not in any convent. Magdalene women are too tired to bother with politics. Trustees had an easy job.

In the dormitory there I was given a partitioned space of my own; I even had a window. It was a moment of pure joy to real-ise that I had that small square of my own, crossed only by my invitation. I unpacked the few things I owned and fitted them around the space.

As I did, a face came around the partition. A girl a little older than me pretended to knock on an imaginary door and made the sound effect with her tongue.

'Howya!' she said with a cheery tone. I glared at her.

She clicked her fingers at me. 'Hello-oh,' she said, shifting her weight onto one leg and crossing her arms. 'Ehh are you deaf or wha?'

I gave her a proper glare, I frowned at her. *Shush.*

'Ehhh,' she said widening her eyes, 'are you alright?'

I pressed my finger to my lips. I was in no humour for pen-ance.

I heard fast footsteps – we had been heard. We were for it now. This stupid bitch had already got me in trouble and I hadn't been here five minutes.

I flashed the whites of my eyes at her. I wished she would just go away.

Miss Hilary came back into the room with a uniform for me folded in her arms.

'What's wrong with you?' this other girl said. She was bra-zen. Miss Hilary headed straight for us.

'Howya, Hills,' the girl said, and she reached out to pat Miss Hilary on the arm as she passed her. Miss Hilary placed the bundle of clothes for me on my bed as I stood in shock.

'Don't get lost in your chat, girls,' she said with a warning look. 'It's nearly tea time and the tablecloths need to be organised first.'

I was so surprised. I thought I had misheard. We could chat?

I turned to the other girl. 'My last place was no talking,' I said.

'Oh gosh,' she said, 'I'd die. I'm a total chatterbox. I'd talk to anyone so I would. I'd die if I couldn't talk.'

I knew what she meant; though I had never been a chatterbox, not being free to speak had almost sent me over the edge more than once. Humans are social animals, even the poorest and most quiet of us.

'I'm Monica, here,' she said, 'Bernie at home. What's your name?'

I said, 'Frances here, Maureen at home.'

'Oh,' she said. She looked at me then like she was trying to suss me out. 'What'll I call you?'

I shrugged. I didn't know anymore.

***

I had never seen a blind person before, and so as I went around the convent that first day, I was nervous to see one. But there was nothing to worry about. I saw a lady walking along the straight corridor with a white stick she used to skirt the space in front of her to check for obstacles. I saw two young women, linking arms as they walked, turn perfectly into the dining room.

I looked at their milky eyes, and how they moved constantly as if they were searching for something to see, and they scared me just for a moment, but then I became so intrigued by how well they moved around the space without help that the fear was gone. I was fascinated. I soon learned that the blind are just as capable in living their lives as any of us.

One woman who lived there knitted the most intricate and beautiful patterns without any mistakes as she sat in her chair in the warmth of the sunlight that came through the tall windows. Others played music. They were incredible.

It was in the blind school, after a while, that I made my first friend, Nora. I called her my friend proudly, and for the first time in my life I felt like I made a connection. She was older than me, possibly forty, and she had a kind face with heavy eyebrows that framed her eyes, which were permanently squeezed shut. She had been in the blind school her whole life, having been dropped in there as a baby once her parents knew she was disabled. That happened a lot back then. She used to chat away to me as I cleaned around her: 'Where are you from? What's it like there? How old are you? Do you like Dublin?' And I felt seen and heard even though my answers were drab: 'Carlow; nothing, really; I think nearly sixteen; I haven't seen much of it.'

'Oh, you should go into town,' she said. 'It's lovely in the city.'

'How on earth do you know that?' I said, surprised into rudeness. But she just laughed and said I should check it out.

I couldn't explain to her that I couldn't leave. I didn't know how to explain what I was. I didn't have money. I didn't have permission to leave the grounds. Nora never pressed it, which I appreciated. Our little friendship remained there, with chitchat. We never talked about much other than the little things.

Once I tried to steal a sweet from a packet she had beside her bed. I didn't make a sound and slipped it into my pocket.

'Put it back, Frances,' Nora said, 'I'm blind, not deaf.'

Well, I was so amazed I didn't even deny it. I just put it back and mumbled a sorry, but then I asked, 'How did you know?'

'I have no sight,' she told me, 'but that's just one of five senses, and I learned to use the others just as well. You see me as disabled, but I am just different; the world has been set up for you … but … well if it was set up for me, which one of us would be disabled?'

My mind was blown. I imagined a world set up for the blind, in darkness with lots of sounds and things to touch – how would I get around?

As I scrubbed the corridors later, I thought about that; how if the world had been designed by someone like my granny, then I wouldn't be here on my knees, a slave. I knew that if my granny was in charge, all kids would be just as loved, and have kindness and soft bodies to sleep on. There'd be no need for my mother to work so hard because she wouldn't have to live with anyone but herself.

Nora told me that day that if I wanted something I should ask for it.

***

I worked in the laundry too, there in the blind school. It was a small laundry just dealing with in-house washing and so it was interesting, with floral blouses and skirts and items that I liked taking care of. There was more handwashing than usual. I used to remark on the quality of the clothes that came through it with the other girls; we would talk about the labels and how much things would cost nowadays in Dublin. We weren't assigned to one machine there. We looked after one batch instead, from start to finish. There were rules, of course, but they were more for safety of the residents and so keeping to them felt good. I took pride in that and was rewarded for it.

I understood why I was asked to mop the floors a certain way, at a certain time, in a certain direction, because the residents were blind and needed to expect things like that. It was a way of caring for them and that suited me. The rules in the other places always felt like such nonsense, made up to hurt us.

But even with the light and warmth and new chat of the blind school, I was still working seven days a week, from early morning till late at night, without pay.

I was still a slave, just in better conditions.

I'd have time to walk the gardens with the other girls, and we would joke that the nuns were watching us out of the triangular windows on either side of the convent. It was a joke, but it was a sign of how stuck we were. We were not free.

On Sundays I could take a walk if I asked, but I would be given a time to go and a time to be back. I wasn't allowed go to the seafront or the beach. I wasn't to walk by the boys' school. I wasn't to talk to anyone or enter a shop.

Sometimes I would go with Miss Hilary to walk the residents and she would let us go down to the seafront. That was so exciting to me, because she always let me hop up on the wall and look at the sea. She always gave me a few minutes there. At the time I thought it was because she needed the little break, because she would sit down with her back to the wall and wait for me, but now I think she saw how much I needed that. She

215

always asked for me when she was walking the residents, that's why I think that. I loved how far away the sea stretched. There was no end, no wall, no locked door. It was the whole world.

One day, on a walk, I stood up on the rocks and stretched my arms out and took the air as deeply into my lungs as I could, like I was trying to pull my soul back into my body from where it was, all the way out there. It felt like I was in a trance.

Two gulls lifted up on a belt of air and swapped sides. One of them tilted his head and looked at me with one eye. I closed one eye and looked back at him. The sun came out and blinded me. I snapped out of it.

'Come on, Frances,' Miss Hilary said, 'let's go back.'

I exhaled my freedom back into the horizon, shoved my hands in my pockets and went back with her.

31

WOMANHOOD

When I got my first period, I had no idea what was happening to me, and I was terrified. I was later than the average, being malnourished and small for my age, and under stress. I first came to know about all of that in the middle of the night, in the dormitory at the blind school in Merrion. I woke up with a dull pain in my abdomen and as I fixed my sheets in bed, attempting to get comfortable, I caught sight of bloodstains on the sheet and on my nightdress and I let out a roar. I clutched at my abdomen, convinced I was stabbed.

'Help me!' I called out. It was dark in the dormitory, save for the moonlight that shone in my window. One by one the heads lifted from the pillows in alarm. Someone turned on the light and everyone sat up.

'Help me!' I screamed again. I wailed, 'I've been stabbed.'

Who had done this to me? Why? I was going to die, I knew it, and I would never get home to see Granny again.

'Was it a man?' The girl in the bed across from me pulled her feet back under herself as if the man might be under her bed. Another girl a few beds down screamed in terror.

Someone pulled the window shut.

'Get help for me!' I screamed. 'Get an ambulance please!'

A few girls ran from the room. One girl came up to me and stood with her hands up around her throat.

'Merciful Heavens, what is going on?' A nun marched in the door, having absolutely none of the scene in front of her, 'Frances, what are you screaming for?'

'I've been killed,' I said, I felt weak hearing the words, 'I'm stabbed through.'

The nun saw the blood and there was a flinch, a moment where she believed me, but then her expression mellowed into impatience. She shook her head, rolled her eyes and took her time coming over to the bed where I was writhing, close to death.

'Frances, go into the bathroom please and wait for me there,' she said, and sent me with a finger in that direction.

I was shocked and appalled. She pulled my hands away from my abdomen, pulled me up by the elbow and shoved me in the direction of the bathroom. Then she followed me in and told me to get into the bath and wash myself.

'You haven't been stabbed, Frances,' she said.

She called through the open door to the other girls to go get some sanitary items, and then, as I sat in the running water, she sat on the side of the bath and told me in clear terms where the blood was coming from. She told me everything was natural, it came on for all women, even Our Lady herself. She spoke at me using words I knew from prayers: wombs, fruit, virgin. I didn't know anything of what she was talking about. She told me that the blood was my cycle and it would come from now on, once a month.

Once I was washed it was clear I hadn't been stabbed at all. The blood was coming out from between my legs. I had vague memories of that happening before, when I was much younger.

The nun gave me pads and I got dressed again.

I was half glad but also half disappointed that I wasn't actually stabbed; to be honest the hospital was still my favourite place I had ever been. I'd wanted to go back.

***

At sixteen I had no idea of money or the world and how it worked. At that age I would have had wages and been managing myself, working out my own budget. For young adults wages are their power, their freedom, I suppose. And I never had that. I was provided with the things I needed, and when I ran out of something, toothpaste or soap, I had to ask for it. When my period came after that, once a month, I would have to ask for sanitary items every time. There was no autonomy in that and I didn't learn how to live. There is something in the psychology of the institution; it breaks you down and keeps you a child. It took me years to learn how to deal with money and organise my own house and finances.

These days I still get a lot of joy out of choosing things for myself, even the smallest of things, because I know what it is like to have no choice.

But even with that, I was in a far better place in the blind school. I had time to breathe – even though the work was hard, you could pause if you needed to, at least. But as I said, we still worked from the early morning until late at night, seven days a week.

Gradually, in my time there, I got given more responsibilities as part of the caring team, and I spent less and less time in the laundry. I had a huge love for caring and it showed, and so eventually my role shifted to the residents' area, where I helped the blind with their day. It was really rewarding. The residents often had visitors and so I would look after tea trays and show their visitors in, opening windows or closing them if it was cold. Most times visitors came it was for a birthday or a special occasion, and during those times a special door was used that was called the 'Outsiders' door'. I would wait by that door ready to open it when the visitors came, wondering who they were and what they felt about leaving their child in this place. I wondered how they didn't know how capable the blind were.

**

I learned how to swim in the blind school. People look at me like I have lost my mind when I tell them I was taught to swim by a blind inmate of the asylum where I scrubbed the floors as an unpaid servant. But it's true.

There was a swimming pool in the asylum for the blind. For all the time I was there I never saw anything going on in it, but I'd imagine they did swimming lessons. I stayed clear of it mostly, as I was afraid of water. I told Nora and she shook her head and wagged a finger.

'Everyone should know how to swim,' she said.

'I'm afraid I'll drown,' I said with as much emotion as I could muster. I didn't even want to talk about it.

'Drowning is the opposite of swimming,' she said. 'Now, let's plan a lesson.'

'I can't!' I said. 'They'll never let me.'

It might have been because she asked, it might have been because she told them she wanted to swim during that time and needed a chaperone, but I was given permission to attend the swimming pool every day with Nora.

The next day I clung to the bar, standing in water up to my knees, dressed in my pants and vest.

'Go in deeper now,' Nora said. I splashed my hands, pretending to do as I was told.

'You didn't move!' Nora said. 'You're still only up to your knees.'

'Are you really blind, Nora?' I said, and she burst out laughing and I did too. My fear subsided a little and I took a few steps further in.

'Who is going to save me if I start drowning?' I shouted at her as the water came up around my thighs. I squealed. What was I doing? My lungs remembered the river water and I started to hyperventilate.

'I will!' she shouted back. 'Calm your breathing, you'll faint!'

'How will you see me under the water?' I said. What was I doing? This was crazy.

I turned to head out, but Nora stopped me with her leg.

'Get in to your waist,' she said. I rolled my eyes and turned back. I got in to my waist.

'Good girl, now go down into the water. Keep your feet on the ground, just get your shoulders wet, okay?' Nora said.

I did it.

'Good woman!' Nora was so pleased with me, it made me feel great. I splashed a little and she let out a whoop.

'Great girl, excellent!'

I was standing in water and you'd think I had won the Olympics with the cheers from my teacher. But it felt amazing to me inside to hear those kinds of words said to me. I wanted more of it. Every move she asked me to make, I made with great enthusiasm. I got mouthfuls of water and sore eyes from the chlorine, but it was worth it to know that I, Maureen Sullivan, was a great girl altogether. It was something I hadn't heard since I was taken from Carlow, taken from my granny.

I learned to swim well, there in the blind school. Driven by a new-found addiction to praise, before long I was striding out in lanes, passing Nora's dangling feet, four times, five, six.

Swimming has been a lovely hobby that I have had since – when I swim I feel like I am flying. I do it as much as I can, thought that's not as often as I'd like. And I still sometimes close my eyes and connect with my other senses, like I did so much in the blind school. I take none of them for granted.

***

The women in the laundry in the blind school weren't silent or downtrodden like in the other places. I was the only one and I soon snapped at least half back to myself, though I am naturally quiet. I thought they must have come from other laundries, like I had, but I never asked. I presumed they too had committed 'crimes' against the patriarchy, but I didn't find out. Maybe some of them had had babies, maybe some of them were being hidden the way I was. I wish I had talked about it. But, regardless, they had lighter hearts than I had, and they forced me to chat and play along with them, even though it was hard for me. I struggled a lot with sleep and was often tired, and I was always on edge. Years of being slapped for no reason will do that to the best of us.

But besides the allowance of conversation, there was no music or relaxation in the blind school. The news was allowed on the radio for the residents to listen to, and so we heard that too. But it was snapped on and snapped off at the start and end of that broadcast. I heard no music at all, except hymns, in my times in the laundries. At least in the blind school we didn't have to work after tea. We were permitted to stand around the kitchen, talking with residents who would come in and out, helping them if they needed us until around eight when we would be instructed to go to our cubicle. Most of the time, having worked all day, we would just go straight to bed and sleep.

There is one time I remember having real fun in the blind school. It was during the middle of the night when the entire convent was asleep. I heard a 'pssst' at the end of my bed and when I sat up, I saw one of the younger women, Bridget, standing there in her nightdress.

'Francesssss,' she hissed.

I told her to shush – I was exhausted and I didn't know what she was doing. She crept around the partition.

'Get up with me, come on,' she said pulling on my hand.

'Where?' I asked.

'Let's go have a laugh, come on,' she said.

I was suspicious. I didn't know what she meant by 'have a laugh'. I didn't think I wanted to find out.

'No,' I said and rolled over. But a minute later she was back with Monica.

'Come on,' they both said. So I sat up and looked at them in the dark. Bridget had a blanket folded under her arm.

'Let's have a bit of fun,' Monica said, and she pulled me up. We crept out of the dorm, past a sleeping Miss Hilary, who was lying with her head back on her arms showing every filling in her head as she snored loudly.

'Right,' said Bridget when we reached the long corridor. She shook out her blanket and handed a corner to me and the opposite corner to Monica. Then she climbed into the middle of it.

'Run that way,' she said, 'drag me and then fire me forward at the same time.'

We looked at her in surprise and then at each other. Would this even work? I was willing to try. We started to run dragging the blanket with Bridget holding on to the other corners of it and then, with a loud one, two, three, we sent her forward down the hall with all our strength. We got the hang of it after a few goes and we took turns. The thrill of being flung along on that blanket was as good as any fairground ride I've taken since. We suppressed our laughter the whole time, which made it funnier, and by the end of it we were in pain from holding it in.

'One last go, then,' Bridget said as I climbed on. The sun was coming up; I could see the beginnings of orange across the rooftops outside.

As I was pulled down the corridor by the two girls, I wished my brothers were there; it had been so long since I'd seen them or had fun with them.

'One ... two ... three ...' They let go but they did it out of sync and instead of straight along I veered off to the side at top speed. I let out a gasp. I was headed straight for the big statue of

Jesus Christ the Sacred Heart that stood on a plinth at the end of the corridor, and I was not stopping.

I swung my body to one side in some vague attempt to stop myself, but I couldn't. I ploughed feet first into the pedestal on which stood a statue of the Sacred Heart. Jesus, with his eyes to heaven and with one hand in prayer, the other clutching his own beating heart, leaned forward and rocked on his flat bleeding feet, once, twice, before descending on top of me with a crash. I tried to catch him, but he bounced, hitting the floor beyond and coming back into my arms as he did.

I sat with the statue between my legs and my eyes couldn't believe what they were seeing. Our Lord was one half on the ground and the other half in my arms. His eyes were still turned up, I supposed to the heavens, but in his two parts in my arms, now he just looked terrified.

I turned my head in absolute shock to see my fellow thrill-seekers clutching at one another in absolute, yet completely quiet, fits of laughter. There was snorts and whines coming from them.

'I'll piss myself,' Monica wheezed.

Bridget had her hands on her knees.

She looked up at me and the broken statue, 'Oh bollix,' she said.

'Bollix,' I said back. I couldn't help but laugh too.

When the funny wore off, and it did, we sat against the wall. Poor Jesus, in pieces, lay where he had fallen.

'What do we do? Stick him back together?' Monica rolled her eyes.

'We don't have glue,' Bridget said.

'There is glue in the residents' room?' I offered.

'That's bloody paper glue. That won't hold him,' Monica scolded, looking at me like I was a fool.

Bridget said, 'Best thing to do is have no idea what happened him ...'

She stood up and dusted herself off, rolled up her blanket and started to walk away. We both stood up too.

She looked over her shoulder. 'Just shrug and say nothing,' she said, shrugging her shoulders, widening her eyes and saying, with her hand on her heart, 'Gosh, Sister, I have no idea how that fell over ...'

Monica said, 'I don't know, Sister, could one of the residents have bumped into it?'

I felt terrible over that line. The blind never bumped into anything. 'Ah ...' I said, 'would you say that though?'

'It's up to them to decide who it was. I won't be giving them clues and you're not to either, Frances. I'm telling you – don't say anything!'

Monica agreed, 'They'll fix that no bother. Just keep it zipped.'

I was asked about the statue. And I kept it zipped. But the Sisters knew it was us. The long stares they gave us as we answered ignorantly were a tell-tale sign. They left the statue lying broken for a few days, possibly to evoke guilt in us, but eventually they sent it for repair and as Monica had said, it came back good as new. It actually looked better, she said, so it was a good thing.

32

THE END OF IT ALL

I was in the blind school at least a year. I know that because I saw all the seasons there. On the last occasion my mother called in, announced by letter the week before.

'My mammy is calling today,' I told everyone.

Nora asked me how she was getting there. I wasn't sure, but perhaps the bus I said. That was my last time talking to Nora.

When my mother arrived, I was called down, and I was never quite sure why, but I was left alone with her. I considered checking on my missing chaperone, but I quite liked the feeling of just me and my mother, beside the window, with a pot of tea I had made and brought up with some biscuits.

Once I realised the nuns were not coming in, I hurriedly ate all of the biscuits.

'Isn't there a nun?' my mother said and we were both surprised. My mouth was full so I shrugged, half smiled and shook my head.

There was a strangely awkward moment, between two people who hadn't had a private conversation in years.

'Is it too cold?' I asked her, noticing her pulling her cardigan closed. She nodded and I stood up to pull the heavy windows down.

'Have you a limp, Maureen?' she asked me, as I was hobbling a little.

'Shoes are too small,' I said.

'You shouldn't wear small shoes, Maureen,' my mother advised me. 'When you get paid, go get some new ones.'

'Mam,' I exclaimed, 'I don't get paid here!'

She stared at me for a minute. Frowned.

'You've great experience of working,' my mother said and then dropped her voice, 'private laundries would be glad of a hard worker like you; they've a cheek not to pay you.'

She whispered the very last part and blessed herself. I thought about it.

'You should ask about it.' My mother drank down her tea. I thought about that. I really should.

As she left, she said, 'Ask about pay.'

So, I did.

The Mother Superior didn't betray her feelings with any expression when the question was put to her the next morning. I'd lost sleep thinking about what my mother had said and I agreed with her. I wasn't a child and I was working my back off for these nuns – the least they could do was pay me something. So I knocked on the Mother Superior's office first thing after doing my morning work and asked her about pay.

'You want pay, Frances?' she said without even looking up.

'I'm sixteen, Sister,' I said. 'I work hard and I should get paid.'

I expected her to argue. Instead, she shuffled some papers and examined them for longer than was polite. She finally looked up at me and straightened her back. Her lips pursed around her clipped tone as she said, 'Frances, nobody is holding you here.'

I was confused. Nobody was holding me? Wait. Yes ... they were. I was held here. The Church was holding me here. *She* was holding me here.

I said, 'Sister, you told me I can't leave though?'

'When did I say that, Frances?'

I couldn't breathe with the horror. I had been brought there the year before. I had been kept there. Given rules and regulations. Was she serious or was this a big joke to them? Had I been free all along?

'Frances, leave us any time you please,' she said, standing and showing me to the door of her office, pushing me through it and closing it behind me.

I wanted to turn around and kick the door back open with such force I'd break her face, but I didn't. Instead, I ran upstairs and sobbed my heart out into the pillow.

Could I have left the last two prisons too? Was I my own warden, keeping myself a prisoner here out of nothing but stupidity?

I imagined myself asking the Mother Superiors in New Ross and Athy, 'Can I leave?' and the thoughts of a positive reply sent shudders through me.

How could she have said it like that? As if it was nothing.

I stood up, pulled my suitcase out from under the head of my bed and crammed my meagre belongings into it, slamming it shut with the anger that boiled inside me.

I went back downstairs and knocked at her door.

'I'm leaving so,' I said.

'Very well. Goodbye, Frances,' she said without even looking up.

I stood there.

'I don't have money for the train,' I said.

She looked up.

'Train to where?' she said.

'Carlow.'

She wrote a note on a paper pad, tore it off and signed it. She handed it to me.

'Go to see Miss Hilary,' she said. 'She will give you the fare.'

I couldn't believe it.

I took the few coins that were handed to me, listened to the directions given to the station and left the convent for good.

As I sat on the train, starving, overwhelmed and with sore feet, I considered the fact that my incarceration was over. The future loomed out before me like the view at Blackrock, and I was both cheered and frightened by it.

A few hours later, I walked up the road in Bennekerry – my first port of call in this new storm – to the little cottage with its windows as bright in the evening sun as the eyes that met mine through them.

EPILOGUE

My granny died in the summer of 1976. I was in London and the police met me on the street as I came back to my council flat with bags of shopping. My mother had called them; none of us had phones you see. I went back to Carlow for the funeral. I had to borrow the money and get the mail boat back, and I barely made it in time.

They had laid granny out in Paddy McGill's funeral parlour in the town. She looked like something from another world, a tiny bird in a wooden box. When I saw her like that, the last light in my tired heart went out.

I didn't come back to Ireland for a long time.

***

Ten years after granny died, thirty-five and married with two children, I tried very hard to end my life. It really seemed to me to be the right thing to do.

You see I had left the Magdalene laundries in 1966, but the truth is, they followed me. When they freed me, I ran back to Carlow, then to London, but I just couldn't get out of that dark tunnel they had locked me in all those years ago. I was still as trapped and as scared as I was in New Ross. I couldn't function as an adult, I didn't know how to, because the years that we learn to negotiate other people, the years we mature, those years were stolen from me. I never had the freedom of my teenage years to experiment and explore human relationships and so I couldn't manage them. I couldn't be in relationships. I didn't know how to open up and I didn't want to, even though my husband begged me to. I had opened up before, I had explained myself and been punished badly for it. That was the lesson I learned at twelve that followed me through my life. I was ashamed.

I should have been talking about my problems, but I could hear those nuns in my ear – *filthy girl* – and I believed those things about myself too, and so pushed my feelings further and further down. The space that was left filled with darkness. I felt as though I was made of shame. It was as though my world became that tunnel. There were walls around me, and there was no light at all, I was stuck. There was no happiness, just a feeling of clawing despair. I held myself tightly closed and it was exhausting. I really believed if people knew what had happened to me as a child, and where I had been as a teenager, that they would be disgusted at me and leave me.

I didn't know joy at all, the place where those feelings come from, I didn't have them. I had dark swirling shadows for a soul.

My husband said to me once that it always felt as if I was on the verge of leaving him, and that he knew if I did I would never come back. He was right. Our marriage never could have survived, even though I did. I woke up in a hospital in London absolutely horrified to find myself still here. Luckily, in those days, in London, if you did anything to harm yourself they didn't let you go until they had something figured out about it. They made me see a counsellor. And perhaps due to exhaustion, I gave up and told on Marty for the second time.

At first I spoke of the things he had done in a sort of code. I couldn't be blunt about it. In fact, I followed that pattern for years, even when I began to speak out about my life. I talked between the lines. Because I was ashamed and I didn't want to make the listeners uncomfortable. It's so sad really, I felt shame and guilt for things done to me by other people, when I was a child. I could never quite get to the point, I fluffed around it. I was still feeling the weight of the punishment that was given to me the first time I confided in someone, the first time I spoke about being abused. I learned that lesson then; the child I was made sure to keep me quiet for most of my life. She was sure that they would send me away again. So I kept things vague, muddled. I didn't want to admit it – I was sexually abused by my stepfather and sent to a Magdalene laundry to ensure nobody found out about it.

In the mid-1990s I was watching the television and I saw a news piece about abuse in the industrial schools. I cannot describe the feeling, seeing people talking about an experience so similar to my own – it brought all of my memories to the surface. I fell apart and a friend suggested I see a healer. Nobody knew why I was how I was, nobody, not even my closest friends, not even my family. I had never once told anyone about Marty and what he did to me, or about the laundry and the hell I was put through.

With my healer, who gave me a sense of safety in her presence that I don't think I had ever known, I started to crawl out of the tunnel I had locked myself into for all of those years. She gave me tools to begin to chip away at the walls, and the light of life started to make its way back through. She encouraged me to spend time with trees and animals and my granny's spirit, and slowly my strength grew. I talked to her, and then I talked to my family and my friends.

Once I found my voice again, I wanted nothing more than to speak out for myself and for other women. I knew that was something I needed to do. Every time I speak, I regain my power. Every time I speak my truth, I silence those inner voices again, and the nuns' whispers fade.

I was abused. I was a victim of child abuse in the family home. I was sent away to protect my abusers and enslaved in the institutions of the Catholic Church. I was trafficked and tortured and my life was destroyed.

What happened to me was wrong, but it still happens in Ireland. One in four Irish people are victims of sexual abuse and yet we still don't talk about it. We need to talk about it.

***

I did go back to New Ross, like I had promised the nuns I would. I was in my fifties. But they were not there. The convent was empty and closed up. The first few times I simply sat in the car and looked at it. Then one day I got out of the car and went in, because the door to the convent church was open. There was a children's day centre being run from there. It was an irony that wasn't lost on me and I ran out around the side. I leant against the outer walls of the corridor from St Aidan's that led to the tunnel under the church, where I had been hidden away, and I felt a huge wash of anger and upset so strong it made me retch. It was such a difficult thing to see young children playing away on the floors that I had scrubbed as a child like them.

Suddenly I knew what it was that I wanted. I wanted to know why. Why had this happened to me? Why was I the one hurt and then punished for it? I felt I had to ask questions and get answers. Then, maybe, I could have peace.

I wrote to the nuns to ask after my records, as an explanation might be in them. At first they didn't respond, then they said they had no records of me in New Ross at all.

I sent them a copy of my Confirmation certificate.

They said they would see me in an office in Limerick and so I went down there. I met with this younger nun who had been given the job of dealing with survivors. She looked me in the eye.

'No children ever worked in the laundries, Maureen,' she lied, 'you were a pupil in St Aidan's.'

I wanted to run away, I wanted to cry. But I stood my ground.

'Show me the ledgers,' I said. 'If I was a pupil, my name will be on those ledgers with all the other children, ticked in and out daily for the classes. Show me my name there.'

She told me she would need time. Things were in storage.

So we arranged a meeting in Kilkenny, in the hotel there. My friend Arnie Stephenson, who was also my boss, came with me – he was a great support. I sat in the lobby across from the same woman who had denied my story last time. We said hello again, she read through prepared items regarding my questions from a folder of papers she had, and I poured tea.

She had not found my name in the ledgers, she said. After a long, awkward silence I said, 'Why did they put me in the laundry? Why not send me to school? I just don't understand.'

Her expression told me she did. She knew why.

Arnie saw it too. 'Maureen has a lot of frustration,' he said, 'and it would help her so much if you could give her any understanding of why she was in the laundry and not the school.'

The nun looked at him and then put her head down. She stared at her notes, moved them around under her fingertips and then she said, 'You must understand ...' she paused and shook her head, 'Maureen was an abused child.'

I didn't understand.

'They believed you could corrupt the innocence ... of the other children,' she said, 'if you mixed with them.'

I heard Arnie gasp.

And then I understood.

'Sister, are you telling me they put me into the laundry and ... all of it ... because they thought I would tell the other children about what my stepfather done to me?'

'It was wrong,' she said, nodding, 'but yes, that's what they did.'

My blood ran cold.

'What happened to you was wrong, Maureen,' the nun said again, and closed her notebook. 'I am sorry.'

The apology meant something. Arnie put his hand on my shaking shoulder and said, 'Let's go, Maureen.'

We were both silent in the car on the way home.

***

It was that apology, however small it was, that gave me the sense of power I wanted for other Magdalene survivors, and I think it was at that moment that my mission began. I wanted to support other women to find their peace in whatever way I could, and when I reached out, I found that they wanted to support me too. I built a new voice for myself through that mission, speaking whenever I was asked to. Eventually I stopped masking my story, the shame fell away and was replaced with bravery. I stopped talking in code and told the truth. And I encouraged others to do the same. We formed an activists' group, and over the years it has grown and become many groups, all with one mission – Justice for the Magdalenes. We have fought together, holding hands to find the strength to hold our heads up to say, 'This should not have happened to us.'

But for all the fighting and exposure and ground we have covered, it still feels like I have more to do. We need to make changes, further than the ones we have made so far. We need to make sure that children are protected, not only in general, but also when they speak up on things that are happening to them. We need to listen and know where the blame should fall. That goes for all children, including teenagers. Girls are blamed in Ireland for wearing leggings, told they are responsible for men's thoughts. Telling girl children to cover up because men will be distracted is not progressive. Telling girls that they are responsible for their own safety, instead of making society a safe place *for* them, is wrong. The way to open this conversation is to start talking about child abuse in louder voices – we need to stop looking away.

I started with healing myself, but I want to help others. That is why I wrote this book. I want to start a conversation that will change things for children like me, and there are children like me all over Ireland. The statistics would horrify you if you dared to look. It makes us all so uncomfortable to acknowledge other people's trauma, and we need to figure out – as a nation – how to sort this out. This is an epidemic and our country won't survive any better than we have if we don't open up.

Recently the group of Magdalene survivors that I'm part of placed a stone at the Little Museum of Dublin to commemorate all of the people who were damaged by the institutions of the Catholic Church in Ireland. It's called the Journey Stone. You can go see it if you'd like to. Placing it felt like the end of something for me. Perhaps I'm ready to leave this world, perhaps I'm finally ready to let go. Everything that I needed to do has been seen through.

I live back in Carlow now, in a house filled with warm light that shines in from the large windows at the back. I live there with my little dog Bella for company. It's a comfortable house, with locks on all the doors and lamps in every corner. I am still afraid of the dark. It's a busy house; my activism means that people come in and out often. In the evenings I try to watch a bit of telly, but it seems that there is always someone to help, someone to comfort. You see, the actions of the nuns back then are like ripples in a lake that can never end, they go on and on. The damage they did to Magdalene women affects their children and their grandchildren. The damage the Catholic Church did to Ireland is still rippling through the people.

Let's start the healing now.

ACKNOWLEDGEMENTS

Maureen Sullivan

I would like to thank the following people who were a great help and support to me in getting my story written.

My children, Michelle Alexander and Jamie Eyles. I'm so grateful to have you both.

My brother Paddy Sullivan, you have been such a support to me and I want to thank you for that. We had a childhood together with bad times and good times, and I am so thankful to have you as my brother.

My co-writer Liosa McNamara. I remember when I was in such a low place and you came down to visit me and said you could write my book, and I never believed we could actually do it, but we did. We had such ups and downs but got through them together. Thank you so much.

My publishers at Merrion Press, Conor Graham, Patrick O'Donoghue, Wendy Logue and Maeve Convery. Thank you for seeing this project to print and for helping me get my story out there.

Olivia Robinson, who died a few years ago, you were always 100 per cent behind me and supported me so much when I first returned to Ireland. You encouraged me to get stronger, and to stand up to it all. I miss you very much. Arnie Stevenson, thank you for always being a powerful strength behind me whenever I had to take hard steps. Thank you for always believing in justice.

Felix O'Neil, thank you for always being on the end of the phone whenever I needed advice or information and for understanding what I have been through with such encouragement.

Thank you also to Eimear Burke, my teacher, for your advice and support, and to the late Howard Campbell, who got me started off with writing my memories down when I was so bad at communication I could barely have a conversation. Both of you helped me to speak.

Audrey Comiskey, my best friend, what would I do without you? You always knew how important it was to get this story out there, for me, and your encouragement has been so valuable. I will never forget it. Thomas Smith, thank you for being a great friend and support, I cherish your memory. Mary Timmons, thank you for all the times I needed someone to talk to and you were there. You are a great friend. Mary Dunleavy, through all the things we have worked on together, all the achievements, we have been so determined in these fights and have got great things done. Well done and thank you for all your support. You're a great woman and a great friend. Mary Furness, thank you for everything that you do, for the way you look after the grave and keep everything going in memory of the Magdalenes. You are a power of strength and I really appreciate your friendship. Mannix Flynn, thank you for all your support and for your fighting spirit and strength to get things done.

I'd also like to remember and thank the late Christine Buckley, all of the people who were held in Magdalene laundries and

Industrial Schools and all the people who have worked with me in my activism and anyone who helped me even in a small way on my journey through life.

Liosa McNamara

Thanks to Mary, my wonderful daughter, and Joe, my lovely son. We are three peas in a pod.

Thanks to Jenny Good for reading the first draft and giving me the boost of confidence I needed at that time.

Huge thanks to Conor, Patrick and all at Merrion Press, and our editor Wendy for her eagle eye and honest feedback.

And, of course, I want to thank Maureen most of all. We have had such a journey together over the past three years. This story is beautiful, honest and sincere because you are. Thank you for your patience and unwavering trust, and for answering the same questions over and over and over again without complaint. It was a privilege to help you tell your story.